REEL
CHARACTERS

Starring
in order of appearance

Elisha Cook

Iris Adrian

Sam Jaffe

Beulah Bondi

Fritz Feld

John Qualen

Charles Lane

Anita Garvin

John Carradine

Rolfe Sedan

Burt Mustin

George Chandler

Great Movie Character Actors

REEL
CHARACTERS

Written and directed by
Jordan R. Young

Produced by
Moonstone Press

In Remembrance

Elliot Bohnen, who kindled my lifelong passion for the cinema
Rose Kaplan, who always gave her grandson a dollar for the movies
Burt Mustin, who befriended a fan who wanted to be a writer

REEL CHARACTERS
Great Movie Character Actors

FIRST EDITION
Published by Moonstone Press,
P.O. Box 142, Beverly Hills CA 90213

Several of the chapters in this book have been revised and expanded from articles which originally appeared in *The Los Angeles Times, The Christian Science Monitor, People on Parade* and *The Los Angeles Herald-Examiner.*

Printed in the United States of America

Cover design by Theodore von Schwarzenhoffen

Typeset by Suzette Mahr, Words & Deeds, Los Angeles, California

Printed by McNaughton & Gunn, Ann Arbor, Michigan

Library of Congress Cataloging in Publication Data
Young, Jordan R.
  Reel characters.

  Includes index.
  1. Moving-picture actors and actresses –United States–Interviews. I. Title.
PN1998.A2Y64 1987   791.43'028'0922 [B]   86-8514
ISBN 0-940410-80-X (alk. paper)
ISBN 0-940410-79-6 (pbk.)

10 9 8 7 6 5 4 3 2 1

Contents

Fritz Feld in *Romance in the Dark* (1938)

Silent Movie (1976)

Foreword

Jordan Young, a devilish creature with a strange smile, approaches his victim very slowly, and starts to ask questions: "When did you come to this country? What was the name of the first motion picture you ever made? In 1948 you appeared in an Abbott and Costello picture called *Mexican Hayride*; how come it was not mentioned in the list of credits you compiled? The name of the Jimmy Stewart film you played in was *The Jackpot*, not *The Game* as you told me."

This inquisitor obviously knows things about my career that I have forgotten!

Here is a young author who cares deeply about preserving the history of the Hollywood character actor. To collect the information for this book he interviewed the actors extensively, in order to get a clear picture of their lives. Jordan not only documents their careers but brings highly personal insight into what kind of people they are — their attitudes, their approach to acting, and their wildly varying experiences with stars and directors.

I am proud to be included among the actors interviewed and particularly happy that someone is documenting the contribution character actors made to the success of films in the Golden Age of Hollywood. The book is full of humor and makes for delicious reading. *My* interview, he did not let me read. Hopefully, he does not tell all!

Dear reader: As the gravedigger in *Hamlet* says, "Go to!" Read it and enjoy!

About the Author

Jordan R. Young is a Los Angeles-based freelance writer-photographer whose work has appeared in *The Los Angeles Times, The New York Times, The Christian Science Monitor, Millimeter, The People's Almanac* and other publications. He is the author of 400 articles and eight books, including *Spike Jones and his City Slickers* and *The Beckett Actor*, the forthcoming biography of actor Jack MacGowran. He is co-author with Bettye Ackerman of the new one-character play, *An Evening with Edna St. Vincent Millay.*

Preface

"I treat every actor as a star, even though the part is small."
—*Frank Capra*

All things considered, I'd rather watch Franklin Pangborn or Edgar Kennedy chew the scenery in a second-rate 1938 movie than sit through most of the entertainment Hollywood is dishing up today — not least because there is precious little screen time for anyone other than the stars.

When I stay up to watch the late show, or rent a video of an old film — and I can look forward to Ned Sparks or Thelma Ritter or Edward Everett Horton in the cast — I know I'm going to enjoy myself that much more.

The character actor was once the backbone of the movie industry. Their faces were often more familiar than their names, but they were no less important than the stars. The Gables and the Garbos brought the money in at the box office, but the players of smaller parts often gave the movies of Hollywood's Golden Era their most indelible moments.

Directors like Frank Capra and Preston Sturges had an unwavering affection for supporting players and always gave them a chance to shine. Sturges created whole scenes that would allow him to use his favorite actors, employing old reliables like William Demarest from one picture to the next.

This book is a portrait of a bygone era, drawn from the vantage point of a dozen of Hollywood's most beloved character actors. Their wry anecdotes and shrewd observations offer what I hope is a rare glimpse behind the tinsel, and a look at films and filmmaking from a fresh point of view.

The actors profiled in this book are more than just familiar faces to me; they're some of the nicest people I've ever met. I've spent long hours in their company, discussing their careers and pouring over their vast collections of memorabilia.

There are many people I would like to have included in this volume. Some, like Billy Gilbert and Mantan Moreland, I met but did not get the chance to interview. Too many others I never got to meet.

When a friend suggested I include Strother Martin in my book, I argued that he was too young. Strother was wonderful, on and off screen — I won't soon forget a chance meeting with him in the supermarket, any more than I could forget him in *Cool Hand Luke*. But I declined to interview him because he was a youngster, compared to the cast of characters I was assembling. I came to regret that decision when he suddenly died of a heart attack at 61.

My thanks to Irv Letofsky (who first suggested this book) and Connie Koenenn of the *Los Angeles Times*, both of whom not only shared my passion for reel characters but happily encouraged it by assigning me to interview a number of them.

I am grateful to Fritz Feld, for his gracious foreword and his perpetual effervescence; Bettye Ackerman, for sharing memories and memorabilia, along with unstinting encouragement; John Cocchi, for his indispensable help in supplementing and proofreading the filmographies; Dick Bann, for letting me pick his archival brain; Mike Hawks, for his unsung talent in ferreting out stills; Helen Chandler, for loaning memorabilia; Marvin Kaplan, Jon Voight and Wim Wenders, for taking time to talk with me.

Thanks are due also to: Doovid Barskin, Jim Beaver, Robert Byron, Elliott Chang, Virginia Christine, Peggy Cook, Jim Curtis, Rich D'Albert, Pen Dennis, Oliver Dernberger, Allen Desmaretz, Jack Dukesbery, Sam Gill, Ben Grego, Ronnie James, Michael Karg, Greg Lenburg, Leonard Maltin, Norman Miller, Estelle Nitikman, Pearle Qualen, Bill Shepard, Chris Simmons, Randy Skretvedt, Red Stanley, Beulah Sedan, Frank Thompson, Sharon Wahl, Pam Young.

Academy of Motion Picture Arts and Sciences; American Broadcasting Company; Anne Schlosser, American Film Institute; Backlot Books; Eddie Brandt's Saturday Matinee; California State University, Fullerton; Columbia Broadcasting System; Columbia Pictures; Cherokee Bookstore; Alan Bunce, *Christian Science Monitor*; Hollywood Poster Exchange; Larry Edmunds Bookshop; Lorimar Productions; Connie Stewart, *Los Angeles Herald-Examiner*; Thomas Lutgen, *Los Angeles Times*; Metro-Goldwyn-Mayer; Monogram Pictures; National Broadcasting Company; National Film Society; Paramount Pictures; Dick Harris, *People on Parade*; RKO Radio Pictures; Hal Roach Studios; Lori Jones and Bob Satterfield, Sons of the Desert; 20th Century-Fox; United Artists; Universal Pictures; Larry Cohen, *Variety*; Walt Disney Productions; Warner Bros. Pictures.

Finally, I am greatly indebted to the subjects themselves, without whose wholehearted and amiable cooperation there would have been no book in the first place. I only wish more of them had lived to see it.

Jordan R. Young
Los Angeles
1986

A Note on the Texts

In the interest of accuracy, much of the information in this book is in conflict with previously published accounts; the subjects themselves were the primary source of such information, including real names and birthdates. While every attempt has been made to verify the statements of those interviewed for this book, the author acknowledges that no memory is infallible, including his own.

A Note on the Filmographies

In 1940, John Carradine and John Qualen gave the finest performances of their respective careers in *The Grapes of Wrath*. The same year, Qualen appeared sans billing in *Brother Orchid*. Carradine topped him the following year, turning up as a bearded extra in a crowd scene, in *All That Money Can Buy* — a stunt that has gone unrecognized by film buffs until now.

The filmographies which follow each chapter are an attempt to list every verifiable appearance on film, including theatrical features, short subjects, documentaries, industrial films, movies made for television and voice-overs. These lists are the most complete ever published for every performer involved. Despite the phenomenal detective work of John Cocchi, however, lists for actors like George Chandler and Rolfe Sedan will never be complete.

Primary references for the filmographies include Call Bureau Cast Sheets, *Film Daily Year Book*, *The New York Times*, *Screen World* and *Variety*, as well as information supplied by the subjects and viewings of the films. Input from readers is welcome and should be addressed to the author in care of the publisher.

Elisha Cook

Elisha Cook exhibited a gift for the gab — and an earthy sense of humor — at our first meeting, in his agent's Hollywood office. If the anecdotes came thick and fast, he was not one to contemplate his craft. A few years later, I was privileged to go camping with him, high in the mountains of northern California. There, at the break of day, he talked introspectively about his beginnings in the theater — and the secrets began to emerge.

A Pulitzer Prize-winning playwright gave Elisha Cook some advice at the outset of his film career that the actor has never forgotten. "Owen Davis Sr. heard I was going to Hollywood. He said to me, 'Junior, you're going to go out there and make a lot of real bad pictures. Now, if you want to be intelligent, play small parts, because then they can never blame you.'

"That's what I've been doing ever since — and I *love* it," declares Cook, whose portrayal of Wilmer, the baby-faced gunsel in *The Maltese Falcon* (1941), has guaranteed him a kind of immortality.

"I've always felt that I could never carry a picture. That takes a talent. Look at the guys and women who starred, and where the hell are they? They're gone. Very few people have that talent, that *real* talent. Bogart had it. Spence [Tracy] had it. Brando had it. You can count them on your fingers."

At 82, Cook has an enthusiasm for life — and work — that belies his age. In a film career that has lasted half a century, he has found a niche for himself in oddball parts — the strange, quiet types whose neuroses simmer under the surface.

"Elisha Cook is the eternal victim, the one that wants to be killed," observes Wim Wenders, who recently directed the veteran actor in *Hammett*. "Strangely enough, there's none of that in him, the little coward, the underdog. Off screen, he is entirely different."

While many actors disdain the roles that make them famous, Cook embraces the disreputable characters that have become his stock in trade. "I love to play pricks," he enthuses. "*The Maltese Falcon*, analyze it — everybody was a shitheel in it. There wasn't one decent person in the whole picture, and look what a film it was. Everyone was a bum. And people, I don't know what it is, they love to watch bums.

13

Just another pretty face — but one *They Won't Forget* (1937).

It's like the guys around the racetrack. They don't want to hear about your winners — but if you've got losers, they want to know about it."

Elisha Cook Jr. was born in San Francisco, December 26, 1903 (not 1902, as often recorded), the son of an actress (Helen Henry) and a theater manager. (He dropped the "Jr." a long time ago, although fans still attach it to his name). His family moved to Chicago when he was a toddler; two weeks later, the 1906 earthquake demolished their former home. He feels he has been living on borrowed time ever since.

Cook was a student in a private boarding school when his mother introduced him to Broadway star Frank Bacon, who was touring in *Lightnin'*. "He said, 'Would you like to go on the stage?'" recalls Cook. "I said, 'Sure, why not?' I sold programs in the lobby and did a walk-on in the courtroom scene for a buck a night. Jason Robards Sr. was the prosecuting attorney."

Bacon then made the 17-year-old neophyte an assistant stage manager on *Thank You*, which toured the country for 105 weeks. "I made more money loading the goddamn baggage car than I did on salary," recalls Cook. "I'd be so damn tired, I'd sleep right in the baggage car, because I had to set up the show in the next town. But I loved it — I got $25 a week for the show; I made $70 loading the baggage.

"I guess I was just naturally drawn to the theater," says Cook, whose father "started and ran all the little theaters" in Chicago. He had no plans to become an actor: "I never thought of stardom either; I just thought of it as work. I went the way everybody did then, stock companies. I played in Waterville, Maine, for six months with the Henry Carleton Players — we were the worst players that have ever been seen. Oh, my god, we were awful. But that's how you got your training."

The apprentice actor learned not only by doing, but by watching. In particular, he remembers a young Barbara Stanwyck, in *The Noose* (1926): "She had a scene — she made me vomit — they were gonna electrocute her husband, and she had a scene with the governor, that she could have the guy's body. I went down to the bathroom and vomited, she was so great in this scene. I'll never forget it. If anybody influenced me, she did."

During his years on the stage, the "perennial juvenile" appeared in such productions as *Henry — Behave* with Edward G. Robinson ("the less said about that the better," noted Robinson in his autobiography); *Kingdom of God* with Ethel Barrymore, *Chrysallis*

With Richard Dix in *The Devil is Driving* (1937).

with Humphrey Bogart and *Three-Cornered Moon* with Ruth Gordon.

Cook was working for $50 a week in a Skowhegan, Maine, stock company when the big break — *Ah, Wilderness!* — came in 1933. "This Harvard professor was directing us. He says, 'Junior, the Theatre Guild wants to see you.' I said, 'You puttin' me on?' He said, 'No. Eugene O'Neill's written a play. They want you to [audition]. You get the hell outta here, go on down there.' I said, 'I gotta have a guarantee I get my job back if they don't hire me.' He said okay.

"I drove all the way to New York in my Model A," recalls Cook. "Now, I walk in the theater, there's George M. Cohan, Gene Lockhart, the whole cast — all but Richard [the young O'Neill]. There's Mr. O'Neill out front. They asked me to read; I read about two pages. O'Neill stood up, he said, 'Wait a minute.' I thought, 'Oh, oh, I'm going back to Skowhegan.' He came down to the footlights and said, 'My cast is complete.' You can imagine how I felt.

"Now, we open in Pittsburgh. O'Neill never went to the theater, except his own plays. We opened on Monday. No Mr. O'Neill. Tuesday, no Mr. O'Neill. Wednesday, the director says, 'Ladies and gentlemen, Mr. O'Neill has seen the play; he wants everybody to remain.' We figured, 'Here it comes, here comes the axe,'" says

Cook. "O'Neill comes backstage, he says, 'This cast is perfect. I'm at fault — 45 minutes comes out of this play.' Of course, Cohan put back in in pauses the 45 minutes O'Neill took out.

"We opened at the Guild Theater in New York and we were a smash hit. About two weeks later there's a knock at my door, it's Mr. O'Neill. He said, 'Junior, I want you to have this' — and he handed me a copy of *Ah, Wilderness!* I said thank you and he walked away. I opened it, and you know what it said? 'To Elisha Cook Jr., who has made my youth live for me forever.'"

Cook's first film was *Her Unborn Child* (1930), a low budget melodrama shot in a garage on New York's Eastside. He was between tours with *Ah, Wilderness!* when Paramount brought him to Hollywood for the first time in 1934 — under a "blanket contract" — to appear with Ida Lupino in *Ready for Love.*

When the actress became ill, the studio assigned him to *Lives of a Bengal Lancer* with Gary Cooper. "In those days, they had seven-year options. I said, 'I'll tell you what. You tear up my contract, I'll do this picture for nothing.' But the picture was for 16 weeks and I had to be back in eight, so I couldn't do it."

The young actor finally made his Hollywood debut two years later as a jockey in *Two in a Crowd.* He tried unsuccessfully to change his billing at the time. "I used 'Elisha Cook Jr.' on the stage, but when I came out to the West Coast I wanted to drop the 'Jr.'," he says. "The studios continued to bill me that way for years. It was stupid — my dad died when I was a kid."

Cookie — as he is known to friends — was still relatively new to the movie business when he did John Ford's *Submarine Patrol*, a film he is not likely to forget. "They had a mock-up of the sub on the backlot at Fox. I'm up on the bridge and they're shooting a big storm sequence. They'd open a chute and thousands of gallons of water would pour out," he explains.

"When they turned the water on I got knocked ass-over-head. I got knocked clear down to the deck — and the piano wire that held up the bridge wrapped around my thumb and cut it off. But these things happen," he says, philosophically. "It's all part of the business. It's what you call line of duty."

The actor still takes chances, but has learned where to draw the line. He allowed the makers of *Baby Face Nelson* to fire live ammunition at him — after being provided with a bullet-proof vest. However, when he was asked to walk into a lion cage in "this terrible, awful picture" called *Black Zoo*, he told the producer, "No way. Get somebody else." The lion trainer who doubled for him was nearly killed.

With Lucille Ball in *Two Smart People* (1946).

Cook has appeared in well over 100 films during the course of his career; he lost count a long time ago. In *The Big Sleep*, he was the stool pigeon who died trying to leak a hot tip to Humphrey Bogart; in *The Killing*, he was the racetrack cashier and henpecked husband of Marie Windsor. In *Voodoo Island*, he was the hapless victim of Boris Karloff, who shrunk him into a doll; in *Rosemary's Baby*, he was the creepy agent renting an apartment to Mia Farrow.

Whether cast as a dope fiend (*Phantom Lady*) or a machine gun-toting grandmother (*A-Haunting We Will Go*), a morgue attendant (*Blacula*) or a stable hand (*Tom Horn*), Cook immerses himself completely in the character. He rarely draws from within: "Only *Ah, Wilderness!* was like me. I don't fuck around with people. And that's the way Mr. O'Neill was.

"I create [the character] the way I think it should be, and then it's up to the director. In the old days, you did exactly what the director said. John Huston would tell you whether you were right or wrong. Humphrey Bogart was a good actor, but he was never a great actor until he got with Huston.

"I was playing Sydney Greenstreet's pimp in *The Maltese Falcon*, right? I want to kill Bogey so badly; I'm so mad I can't see straight. We were doing the scene and Mary Astor said, 'Cookie, listen, just let

18

With Claire Trevor and Lawrence Tierney in *Born to Kill* (1947).

the tears come.' And that's exactly what happened," he remembers. "You know what Huston wanted to do? He wanted to put fake eye-lashes on me. Wouldn't that have been great? But he said, 'No, I'd better not go that far.'"

It was that film which made not only Cook's reputation, but Huston's as well. "It was John's first picture," says Cook. "He wanted to shoot one scene without a cut — the one where we're all in the room and I'm beggin' Greenstreet to let me kill Bogart.

"Now John wants this in one shot — never been done before. So he said, 'We're going to close down and rehearse this for a day or two.' Jack Warner heard about it; he came down on the set. He said, 'No way you're going to close down in my studio for two days.' So Huston and Bogart walked off the set. That shot runs 950 feet without a cut — 10 minutes of film."

In another classic of the detective genre, *The Big Sleep*, Cook uttered "the greatest line I've ever had" — thanks to director Howard Hawks. "These bums are beating the crap out of Bogey in the alley and I'm standing there watching them and I don't do anything," he notes. "I take him upstairs, he's washing up and he says, 'What the hell kind of man are you?' And Hawks just came up with this line — I said, 'Listen, when a guy's doing a job I don't kibitz.'"

His favorite movie, however, remains Stanley Kubrick's imaginative race track heist caper — and first feature — The Killing: "Stan's script was so original it startled people. I said, 'This is gonna be a sensation.' Nobody believed me; not even Sterling Hayden, who starred in it. And you know where Stan went from there." Kubrick later sent for the actor when he was doing Lolita in England, but British Equity wouldn't allow Cook to work there.

Perhaps the biggest disappointment of the actor's career remains Damon Runyon's Little Pinks. RKO wanted a star for the title role — a timid busboy infatuated with a nightclub singer — but Runyon insisted on Cook. The studio agreed, on the condition that Carole Lombard could be signed to co-star. When the actress was killed in a plane crash, Henry Fonda and Lucille Ball were eventually cast in the film (retitled The Big Street).

Much to his regret, Cook has returned to the stage only twice in recent years. In 1963, he played the Goebbels counterpart in the ill-fated Broadway production of Brecht's Arturo Ui. A 1980 Texas dinner theater presentation of Arsenic and Old Lace featured him as Dr. Einstein.

Cook has become a familiar face to television audiences over the years, appearing in such series as The Honeymooners, Gunsmoke, Star Trek and Baretta. During the 1985-86 season he appeared on The Fall Guy, The A-Team, the new Twilight Zone and Magnum, P.I., in which he has the recurring role of Icepick.

Moviegoers have seen him in recent years as the corner man in the remake of The Champ, an unscrupulous old carnival barker in Carny and a down-and-out war veteran in Harry's War. In Hammett, he had a meaty role as the taxi driver who chauffered Maltese Falcon author Dashiell Hammett (Fredric Forrest) around San Francisco.

Being in demand has little to do with his skill as an actor, contends Cook. "You get lucky now and then," he says. "When you freelance, things overlap; you have a chance to do another picture but you're still shooting and you can't do it. It happened that Keith Merrill, who wrote and directed Harry's War, rearranged his whole schedule so I could fly to Savannah and do Carny. That's what I call luck. Who else would do that?"

There was a point in the early 1950s where Cook found himself out of luck — and out of work — after getting into a fight with the studios over his salary. Rather than work for scale, he took a laborer's job, shoveling gravel on the Owens Valley pipeline in Northern California for a year and a half.

As a vengeful ex-con in CBS' *The Millionaire* (1957).

He was beginning to wonder if he would ever act again when he was cast in *Shane*, as a proud and defiant homesteader who is gunned down by Jack Palance. It was one of the few opportunities he has had to play a good guy in his long and distinguished career: "I'm laying in the mud and George Stevens, the director, comes up to me. You know what he said? 'You dumb sonuvabitch, see what happens when you stand up for a principle.'"

For all his experience, Cook still has sleepless nights when preparing a role, "even if it's just a lousy TV show. You're trying all the time to create something that's right. It might stink, but you're still trying to do the best you can."

Jon Voight, who received ringside first aid from Cook in *The Champ*, marvels, "He makes mistakes like a young actor, he jumps in with both feet. Elisha is not afraid to experiment. He has no gimmicks; he doesn't protect himself," contends Voight. "He's great playing weasels and cowards, but he's just the opposite in life. Elisha will take the first punch — he has no fear at all."

Between acting jobs, Cook retreats to his home in Bishop, California, 300 miles from Hollywood. He spends much of his time camping and fishing at nearby Lake Sabrina, nestled high in the Sierra Nevadas. "I could spend the rest of my life up here — it's an absolute paradise," says Cook, who lives with his wife Peggy, a former stand-in for actress Carole Landis. In the spring of 1986 they celebrated their 43rd anniversary.

Clearly, his attitude about the precarious nature of the actor's life helps keep Cook young and vigorous. "My agreement, with all the agents who have handled me over the years, is that they never tell me anything at any time about Hollywood — I don't care what it is — unless it's firm. Otherwise I don't want to know about it.

"I love this business," he states. "It makes people happy. Most people have such humdrum lives, they've gotta have an outlet — and the movies are a great outlet." He himself hasn't seen a film in years: "I never look at 'em. I get embarrassed when I see myself," he says. "What they do with it once my part is done doesn't interest me, 'cause I have nothing to do with that end of it."

If Cook has reached the point where he can afford to be choosy about the parts he plays, he disregards the option. "I don't worry about scripts or parts," he claims, "as long as they pay me. To me, the worst thing in the world is to retire. As long as they want me, I'll work. A while back I asked my manager if I should quit. He said, 'No way. You've got a lot of mileage left on you.'"

photo by the author

"I'm the biggest goldbrick Hollywood's ever known."

THE FILMS OF ELISHA COOK

Cook did not appear in BULLETS OR BALLOTS (1936) or THE ESCAPE ARTIST (1982), as recorded elsewhere. A film clip of Cook was used in the documentary, GEORGE STEVENS: A FILMMAKER'S JOURNEY (1985).

Shorts

KILL OR BE KILLED — U.S. Army-Warner Bros. 1943 [combat film]
KIDNAP EXECUTIVE STYLE — Brose Productions 1975 [educational]
SENIOR POWER AND HOW TO USE IT — Brose Productions 1978
   [educational]
SMART ABOUT MONEY — Brose Productions 1979 [educational]
HOME SECURITY — Brose Productions 1979 [educational]
OUT AND ABOUT — Brose Productions 1979 [educational]
SAFE ON THE STREETS — Brose Productions 1979 [educational]

Features

HER UNBORN CHILD — Windsor Picture Plays 1930
TWO IN A CROWD — Universal 1936
PIGSKIN PARADE — 20th Century-Fox 1936
LOVE IS NEWS — 20th Century-Fox 1937
BREEZING HOME — Universal 1937
THEY WON'T FORGET — First National 1937
DANGER! LOVE AT WORK — 20th Century-Fox 1937
THE DEVIL IS DRIVING — Columbia 1937
LIFE BEGINS IN COLLEGE (Life Begins at College) —
   20th Century-Fox 1937
WIFE, DOCTOR AND NURSE — 20th Century-Fox 1937
MY LUCKY STAR — 20th Century-Fox 1938
SUBMARINE PATROL — 20th Century-Fox 1938
THREE BLIND MICE — 20th Century-Fox 1938
NEWSBOY'S HOME — Universal 1939
GRAND JURY SECRETS — Paramount 1939
HE MARRIED HIS WIFE — 20th Century-Fox 1940
STRANGER ON THE THIRD FLOOR — RKO Radio 1940
PUBLIC DEB NO. 1 — 20th Century-Fox 1940
TIN PAN ALLEY — 20th Century-Fox 1940
HELLZAPOPPIN' — Universal 1941
LOVE CRAZY — MGM 1941
SERGEANT YORK — Warner Bros. 1941
BALL OF FIRE — Goldwyn-RKO Radio 1941
THE MALTESE FALCON — Warner Bros. 1941
MAN AT LARGE — 20th Century-Fox 1941

With Jack Oakie and John Payne in *Tin Pan Alley* (1940).

I WAKE UP SCREAMING (Hot Spot) — 20th Century-Fox 1941
A GENTLEMAN AT HEART — 20th Century-Fox 1942
A HAUNTING WE WILL GO — 20th Century-Fox 1942
SLEEPYTIME GAL — Republic 1942
MANILA CALLING — 20th Century-Fox 1942
WILDCAT — Paramount 1942
IN THIS OUR LIFE — Warner Bros. 1942
PHANTOM LADY — Universal 1944
CASANOVA BROWN — International-RKO Radio 1944
UP IN ARMS — Goldwyn-RKO Radio 1944
DARK WATERS — United Artists 1944
DARK MOUNTAIN — Paramount 1944
DILLINGER — Monogram 1945
WHY GIRLS LEAVE HOME — PRC 1945
CINDERELLA JONES — Warner Bros. 1946
JOE PALOOKA, CHAMP — Monogram 1946
THE FALCON'S ALIBI — RKO Radio 1946
THE BIG SLEEP — Warner Bros. 1946
TWO SMART PEOPLE — MGM 1946
BLONDE ALIBI — Universal 1946
BORN TO KILL — RKO Radio 1947
THE LONG NIGHT — RKO Radio 1947
THE GANGSTER — Allied Artists 1947

As a veteran carnival barker in *Carny* (1980).

FALL GUY — Monogram 1947
THE GREAT GATSBY — Paramount 1949
FLAXY MARTIN — Warner Bros. 1949
BEHAVE YOURSELF! — RKO Radio 1951
DON'T BOTHER TO KNOCK — 20th Century-Fox 1952
SHANE — Paramount 1953
I, THE JURY — United Artists 1953
THUNDER OVER THE PLAINS — Warner Bros. 1953
SUPERMAN'S PERIL — 20th Century-Fox 1954 [comprised of 1953
     Superman TV episodes]
DRUM BEAT — Warner Bros. 1954
THE OUTLAW'S DAUGHTER — 20th Century-Fox 1954
TIMBERJACK — Republic 1955
TRIAL — MGM 1955
THE INDIAN FIGHTER — United Artists 1955
THE KILLING — United Artists 1956
ACCUSED OF MURDER — Republic 1956
THE LONELY MAN — Paramount 1957
BABY FACE NELSON — United Artists 1957
CHICAGO CONFIDENTIAL — United Artists 1957
VOODOO ISLAND — United Artists 1957
PLUNDER ROAD — 20th Century-Fox 1957
HOUSE ON HAUNTED HILL — Allied Artists 1958
DAY OF THE OUTLAW — United Artists 1959

PLATINUM HIGH SCHOOL — MGM 1960
COLLEGE CONFIDENTIAL — Universal 1960
ONE-EYED JACKS — Paramount 1961
JOHNNY COOL — United Artists 1963
THE HAUNTED PALACE — American International Pictures 1963
BLACK ZOO — Allied Artists 1963
PAPA'S DELICATE CONDITION — Paramount 1963
BLOOD ON THE ARROW — Allied Artists 1964
THE GLASS CAGE (Den of Doom) — Futuramic Releasing 1964
THE SPY IN THE GREEN HAT — MGM 1966 [comprised of *Man From UNCLE* TV episodes; no U.S. theatrical release]
WELCOME TO HARD TIMES — MGM 1967
ROSEMARY'S BABY — Paramount 1968
THE GREAT BANK ROBBERY — Warner Bros.-Seven Arts 1969
EL CONDOR — National General 1970
THE MOVIE MURDERER — Universal-NBC 1970 [TV movie]
NIGHT CHASE — Cinema Center-CBS 1970 [TV movie]
THE NIGHT STALKER — ABC 1972 [TV movie]
THE GREAT NORTHFIELD, MINNESOTA RAID — Universal 1972
BLACULA — American International Pictures 1972
EMPEROR OF THE NORTH — 20th Century-Fox 1973
PAT GARRETT AND BILLY THE KID — MGM 1973 *scenes deleted*
THE OUTFIT — MGM 1973
ELECTRA GLIDE IN BLUE — United Artists 1973
STEELYARD BLUES (The Final Crash) — Warner Bros. 1973
THE PHANTOM OF HOLLYWOOD — CBS 1974 [TV movie]
THE BLACK BIRD — Columbia 1975
MESSIAH OF EVIL — International Cine Film Corp. 1975
WINTERHAWK — Howco International 1975
ST. IVES — Warner Bros. 1976
MAD BULL — Filmways-CBS 1977 [TV movie]
DEAD OF NIGHT — NBC 1977 [TV movie]
THE CHAMP — MGM-United Artists 1979
1941 — Uni-Columbia 1979
SALEM'S LOT — Warner Bros.-CBS 1979 [TV movie]
TOM HORN — Warner Bros. 1980
CARNY — Lorimar-United Artists 1980
HARRY'S WAR — Taft International 1981
LEAVE 'EM LAUGHING — Charles Fries-CBS 1981 [TV movie]
TERROR AT ALCATRAZ — Universal-NBC 1982 [TV movie]
HAMMETT — Zoetrope-Orion-Warner Bros. 1983
THIS GIRL FOR HIRE — Orion-CBS 1983 [TV movie]
NATIONAL LAMPOON GOES TO THE MOVIES (National Lampoon's Movie Madness) — MGM-United Artists 1983 [no theatrical release]
OFF SIDES (Pigs vs. Freaks) — Ten-Four Productions-NBC 1984 [TV movie]
IT CAME UPON THE MIDNIGHT CLEAR — Columbia 1984 [TV movie]

Iris Adrian

Getting Iris Adrian to sit still long enough for something resembling an interview was like trying to corral a jackrabbit. When I finally managed to pin her down, I found her as brash and sassy in person as on screen, and far more colorful. Her voice was as loud as her attire (a shocking pink dress and matching hat); her remarks about her career were often punctuated with raucous laughs, of the kind generally reserved for wild parties.

For all the big mouth dames she played on screen, Iris Adrian never talked back to her directors. She did was she was told to do and simply hoped she did it right. "If you didn't," she says, "they let you know quick.

"We used to have the meanest directors in the world. They all had accents, and they all had laryngitis," asserts Adrian, who has become the epitome of the tough, wisecracking blonde during six decades in show business. Her Hollywood career — she has appeared in over 125 films — has been "all roses — but, oh, those thorns!

"The directors weren't too polite in those days: 'What the hell are you doing? Do it this way, you dumb sonuvabitch!' But I wasn't hurt; I was used to that because I came up in the chorus. I was often scolded by my mother, and when I went into show business, it was the same thing. They'd scream, 'Hey you idiot, third from the right!' I'd say, 'Oh, that's me.'

"I didn't mind," says Iris. "You know where you are with a screamer. Directors are so polite now. It isn't as good today... with these guys you don't know where the hell you are. 'You idiot!' or 'You jerk!' is better than 'Miss Adrian.'"

Iris Adrian Hostetter (not Hofstadter, as often recorded) was born May 29, 1912 (not 1913) in Los Angeles. She was a 13-year-old Hollywood High School student when she got her start, by winning a perfect back contest. On the advice of a fellow contestant, she then auditioned for — and won — a spot in the chorus of Larry Ceballos' Revue. She changed her name to Jimmie Joy, but soon switched back to Iris Adrian.

What inspired her to go into show business? "Money," she says, bluntly. "I didn't have any idea [of a career]. It was the Depression,

29

everybody was starving to death, and I got a job. They said, 'We can use you,' and I went."

Iris, whose mother did extra work in silent films, has only a vague recollection of her beginnings. Though she recalls being under contract to Paramount as a chorus girl "maybe as early as 1926" — and reportedly did some two-reel color shorts for MGM — the earliest evidence she has of her film career is a photo of herself with Jean Harlow in a 1928 Charley Chase comedy.

While she appeared with Maurice Chevalier in the all-star *Paramount on Parade*, and other films, she was active primarily in stage shows at that point in her career. Among the earliest were *Bambina*, and two for Fred Waring — *Rah Rah Daze* and *The New Yorkers*, which took her to the East Coast.

The latter engagement led to Florenz Ziegfeld's 1931 *Follies*, and then *Hot-Cha!* (Ziegfeld wanted to call it *Laid in Spain*). Iris, who

Iris (second from right) with Jean Harlow (fourth from left), Kalla Pasha (kneeling) and Charley Chase in *Chasing Husbands* (1928).

earned the nickname of "The Girl With the Million-Dollar Figure" during that period, also found work in New York at Nils T. Granlund's Hollywood Restaurant. While there she was featured with Rudy Vallee and his Connecticut Yankees.

A screen test — in which she did "my version" of *Anna Karenina* — won her another contract with Paramount in 1934. "George Raft saw me at the Hollywood Restaurant and wanted me to travel with him in his show. I danced with him all across the country," she says. "Paramount wanted me too; that was the way they got me back to Hollywood without paying my fare."

She detested the picture she made with Raft at the end of the tour (*Rumba*) but later worked with him on another film — *Broadway* — that she regards as her personal favorite. "Raft was a wonderful fellow," she says. "He always had a romance somewhere in another city.

"People worked all the time. They were never with the person they loved; they were always on the phone," she muses. "I've had a few romances in my life, a few marriages [four]. Every time I married somebody I went out on the road and never saw them again; they became a bachelor when they married me."

Iris returned to New York frequently in the 1930s for stage and nightclub work. "I had to go where the job was," says Adrian, whose talents were much in demand at popular New York nightclubs like Leon and Eddie's. She still remembers the night Stan Laurel came in: "He'd picked up a lot of dames on the way, and they were all drinking. They heckled me all night," she reports.

The night spots Adrian worked were also frequented by gangsters. "They were so kind to us, we just loved them," she says. "Charlie Lucky once said to me, 'If you ever go wrong, I've got a job for you.' I didn't know what the hell he meant — they had a whore house. If all the Follies girls would've done it for nothing," she notes, "they wouldn't have been in business."

Iris herself played a woman of loose morals picked up by Laurel and Hardy in *Our Relations* — one of her early films. "It's funny," she says. "You just get together and do it. Later people say, 'How was it?' You don't remember; you just did it. I don't know whether it was so much fun or not. What the heck is to enjoy? You just go to work."

Her recollection of working with Marx Brothers in *Go West* — as a saloon girl — is equally brusque. "They didn't get along so well with each other," she observes. "One day one of them was late and the next day the other two were late. The director said, 'It's like working with kids.' Same thing with Abbott and Costello."

Iris (right) is wooed by Oliver Hardy in *Our Relations* (1936), as Lona Andre and Stan Laurel look on.

In 1938 Iris returned to the stage as a strip-tease dancer, in Kaufman and Hart's *The Fabulous Invalid*. George S. Kaufman himself taught her the striptease. "I had never seen one," she says. "I didn't have a chance to go to the theater — I was *in* the theater. I wanted to have a little life of my own, but all I did was work — I slept about two hours a night."

The following year Iris took over the lead in *I Must Love Someone* on two day's notice, then toured in *Of Mice and Men*. "I'd rather hide under a rock [than go on stage]," she confesses, "but I couldn't afford to. Pictures were a cinch; I was never frightened of the camera. But opening night on the stage — you look out there, they're all dressed up. They've come to see you and you think, 'Jeezus, I'm not worthy of them.'"

While she was often typecast as a showgirl or a moll, Adrian's talents were in constant demand: "I sometimes did two films in one day," she says. She appeared opposite many of the top stars in Hollywood, but there are few she recalls with any particular fondness.

"I worked all the time, but I never paid much attention. When I was through, I got paid and beat it," says Iris. "They tell you all the stars are great. They ain't — nobody is. I'm not either," she says, mockingly. "I always liked people, but I don't think some of the people I worked with did. I didn't hang around long enough to find out."

With June MacCloy (center), Joan Woodbury and Groucho Marx in *Go West*
(1940).

Adrian stuck around long enough to work with some of filmdom's
most prominent directors, though — and collected indelible impres-
sions of them. Michael Curtiz, who directed her in three pictures
including *Flamingo Road*, "made my life miserable," she says. "He was
the meanest... I kept saying, 'Why did you hire me?' He'd say,
'Because I love you.' Oh god, he was mean. Imagine if he hated me!"

"Fritz Lang was another screamer. Ernst Lubitsch would really let
you have it. They all had accents and laryngitis. They'd always have
some assistant come over and say, 'Get everything exactly right
today. He has laryngitis and he doesn't want to scream at you.'
Rouben Mamoulian was another one; he was viciously mean. The
others were mean, but there was an undercurrent of friendship."

Jerry Lewis, who cast her in *The Errand Boy* — as an elegantly-
dressed movie star who gets showered with champagne — was "a
super guy," she says. "When I first got the call I thought, 'Oh, no!'
But I had a wonderful time on his set. He'd do the whole thing for you,
and say, 'That's what I want' — which is marvelous. He was mild,
compared to what I'm used to," says Iris.

Another director she recalls fondly is William Wellman, who cast
Adrian in *Lady of Burlesque* as a stripper in a second-rate burlesque
house. He also gave her the memorable role of bad, blonde Two-Gun
Gertie in his zany 1942 comedy, *Roxie Hart*.

33

As Two-Gun Gertie in *Roxie Hart* (1942) — "That's just me."

(Adrian had a role akin to Gertie in *Flamingo Road* — and a line of dialog that virtually summed up her film career. When Joan Crawford asks what she's doing in jail, Iris retorts, matter-of-factly, "My boy friend stabbed himself on a knife I was holding.")

Asked how she developed the character of the tough broad she essayed to perfection in *Roxie Hart* and other films, the actress replies, "That's just me, I guess. I never planned anything. You ask yourself, 'How are you going to play this? Same way you did everything else.'

"I saw me the other day in *The Paleface* with Bob Hope," she observes. "Loved it. Years ago [I'd think] 'I should've done this' — but now, it's perfect. Just love that broad — 'cause I don't even know her any more; she's gone from me. I couldn't remember anything about what the hell she was up to then."

If there is one personality that stands out in Adrian's memory, it is Jack Benny, whose act she joined in 1952. "Jack was probably the greatest thing that ever hit the planet. He was so dear. He'd say terrible things: 'Iris Adrian... you expect a beautiful girl to walk out and out comes *Iris.*' He was horrible to me but I liked it. I like to be mistreated," she says with a laugh. "I was with Benny when I hit 40. It was *awful.* You know, trying to be cute and 40, it's terrible. Jack felt sorry for me and everything. I was still with him when I hit 60 . Jack said, 'Oh, my God. When you were 40 you had us all in tears. Now it's 60? Are you going to drive me nuts every 20 years?'

"I can't believe he's gone. He was the dearest man in the world and he never lost his temper. I was always trying to get a compliment; I never got one in 20 years," says Adrian, who played an obnoxious waitress on Benny's radio show and one of the kooky Smithers Sisters in his nightclub act. "He never said, 'You're marvelous.' He said, 'When things aren't right, I'll tell you. And I'll probably *fire* you at the same time.'"

Although there have been few roles in recent years for actresses of her vintage, Iris has been more active than she would prefer. Walt Disney Productions put her talents to work constantly in the 1970s, until the sudden switch in their image; she did ten pictures at the studio, beginning with the role of a landlady in *That Darn Cat.* In *Scandalous John* she was featured as Mavis, "an old bar room broad" who runs a desert watering hole.

"People like Iris Adrian give so much of a dimension to the stars of a picture," observed former Disney casting director Bill Shepard. "I think it's a good idea to use her rather than somebody who doesn't add that extra dimension. She makes the stars look better."

With Frank Fontaine and Jack Benny.

Another fan is Burt Reynolds' producer, Hank Moonjean, who cast her in *The End* (her scene was later cut) and subsequently in *Paternity* — her most recent film. "He said, 'Send me a picture,' she notes, 'so I sent him one. I said, 'This picture is eight years old. I look just like this, only worse.'"

Television audiences have seen Iris as the wise-cracking receptionist on the short-lived *Ted Knight Show*, and more recently on the new *Love, American Style*. Despite her claim that she doesn't want to work any more, she appeared on *Love Boat* early in 1986.

"It's time to retire. I don't know how much time I've got left on this planet," says the recently-widowed actress, whose last husband — one-time football star Ray "Fido" Murphy — "deserted" after 33 years of marriage.

"I'm retired now; I don't have an agent. I don't want to go on all those job interviews — my God, I might get 'em!" she says, with a throaty laugh. "When you're young you have a future to look forward to. I have no future; it's my last act. I don't need the money, so the hell with it. Why get up at 6 o'clock in the morning and bother with it all?"

As Mavis in Disney's *Scandalous John* (1970).

THE FILMS OF IRIS ADRIAN

Adrian may have worked at Paramount as early as 1926, though there is no evidence to substantiate this. Titles for other shorts in which Iris appeared are unavailable at present. She reportedly appeared in the documentary, CITY OF CONTRASTS (1931); she does not appear in DEVIL'S HARBOR (1954), as recorded elsewhere. Based on a list compiled by John Cocchi, and other sources.

Shorts

CHASING HUSBANDS — Roach-MGM 1928
THE FRESHMAN'S GOAT — Christie-Educational 1930
COLLEGE CUTIES — Christie-Educational 1930
TEARING TO GO — Christie-Educational 1930
IF I'M ELECTED — Vitaphone-Warner Bros. 1932
MAN TO MAN — Educational-20th Century Fox 1937
HOW TO CLEAN HOUSE — RKO Radio 1948
FOY MEETS GIRL — Columbia 1950
SO YOU WANT TO KNOW YOUR RELATIVES — Warner Bros. 1954
SO YOU WANT TO BE PRETTY — Warner Bros. 1956

Features

PARAMOUNT ON PARADE — Paramount 1930
LET'S GO NATIVE — Paramount 1930
RUMBA — Paramount 1935
STOLEN HARMONY — Paramount 1935
GAY DECEPTION — Fox 1935
MURDER AT GLEN ATHOL (Criminal Within) — Invincible 1936
GRAND EXIT — Columbia 1935
A MESSAGE TO GARCIA — 20th Century-Fox 1936
OUR RELATIONS — Roach-MGM 1936
ONE RAINY AFTERNOON — United Artists 1936
STAGE STRUCK — First National 1936
MISTER CINDERELLA — Roach-MGM 1936
LADY LUCK — Chesterfield 1936
GOLD DIGGERS OF 1937 — First National 1936
ONE THIRD OF A NATION — Paramount 1939
BACK DOOR TO HEAVEN — Paramount 1939
GO WEST — MGM 1940
MEET THE WILDCAT — Universal 1940
THE LADY FROM CHEYENNE — Universal 1941
HORROR ISLAND — Universal 1941
MEET THE CHUMP — Universal 1941
ROAD TO ZANZIBAR — Paramount 1941

WILD GEESE CALLING — 20th Century-Fox 1941
SING ANOTHER CHORUS — Universal 1941
TOO MANY BLONDES — Universal 1941
NEW YORK TOWN — Paramount 1941 *scenes deleted*
HARD GUY — PRC 1941
I KILLED THAT MAN — Monogram 1941
SWING IT, SOLDIER — Universal 1941
ROXIE HART — 20th Century-Fox 1942
RINGS ON HER FINGERS — 20th Century-Fox 1942
TO THE SHORES OF TRIPOLI — 20th Century-Fox 1942
BROADWAY — Universal 1942
FINGERS AT THE WINDOW — MGM 1942
JUKE BOX JENNY — Universal 1942
ORCHESTRA WIVES — 20th Century-Fox 1942
MOONLIGHT MASQUERADE — Republic 1942
HIGHWAYS BY NIGHT — RKO Radio 1942
THUNDER BIRDS — 20th Century-Fox 1942 *scenes reshot with
    Joyce Compton*
McGUERINS FROM BROOKLYN (Two Mugs From Brooklyn) —
    Roach-United Artists 1942
CALABOOSE — Roach-United Artists 1943
THE CRYSTAL BALL — Paramount-United Artists 1943
HE'S MY GUY — Universal 1943
LADIES' DAY — RKO Radio 1943
TAXI, MISTER — Roach-United Artists 1943
LADY OF BURLESQUE (The G-String Murders) — United Artists 1943
ACTION IN THE NORTH ATLANTIC — Warner Bros. 1943
CAREER GIRL — PRC 1943
SUBMARINE BASE — PRC 1943
HERS TO HOLD — Universal 1943
SPOTLIGHT SCANDALS — Monogram 1943
HIS BUTLER'S SISTER — Universal 1943
SHAKE HANDS WITH MURDER — PRC 1944
ONCE UPON A TIME — Columbia 1944
THE SINGING SHERIFF — Universal 1944
MILLION DOLLAR KID — Monogram 1944
SWING HOSTESS — PRC 1944
THE WOMAN IN THE WINDOW — RKO Radio-International 1944
ALASKA — Monogram 1944
I'M FROM ARKANSAS — PRC 1944
BLUEBEARD — PRC 1944
IT'S A PLEASURE! — RKO Radio-International 1945
ROAD TO ALCATRAZ — Republic 1945
STEPPIN' IN SOCIETY — Republic 1945
BOSTON BLACKIE'S RENDEZVOUS (Surprise in the Night) —
    Columbia 1945

With Barry Fitzgerald and Betty Hutton in *The Stork Club* (1945).

THE STORK CLUB — Paramount 1945
VACATION IN RENO — RKO Radio 1946
THE BAMBOO BLONDE — RKO Radio 1946
CROSS MY HEART — Paramount 1946
FALL GUY — Monogram 1947
PHILO VANCE RETURNS — PRC 1947
LOVE AND LEARN — Warner Bros. 1947
THE WISTFUL WIDOW OF WAGON GAP —
    Universal-International 1947
THE TROUBLE WITH WOMEN — Paramount 1947
OUT OF THE STORM — Republic 1948
SMART WOMAN — Allied Artists 1948
THE PALEFACE — Paramount 1948
THE LOVABLE CHEAT — Film Classics 1949
MISS MINK OF 1949 — 20th Century-Fox 1949
FLAMINGO ROAD — Warner Bros. 1949
MY DREAM IS YOURS — Warner Bros. 1949
MIGHTY JOE YOUNG — RKO Radio 1949
WOMAN ON PIER 13 (I Married a Communist) — RKO Radio 1949
SKY DRAGON — Monogram 1949
TRAIL OF THE YUKON — Monogram 1949

TOUGH ASSIGNMENT — Lippert Pictures 1949
ALWAYS LEAVE THEM LAUGHING — Warner Bros. 1949
THERE'S A GIRL IN MY HEART — Allied Artists 1949
BLONDIE'S HERO — Columbia 1950
JOE PALOOKA IN HUMPRHEY TAKES A CHANCE — Monogram 1950
SIDESHOW — Monogram 1950
ONCE A THIEF — United Artists 1950
HI-JACKED — Lippert Pictures 1950
MY FAVORITE SPY — Paramount 1951
STOP THAT CAB — Lippert Pictures 1951
VARIETIES ON PARADE — Lippert Pictures 1951
THE RACKET — RKO Radio 1951
G.I. JANE — Lippert Pictures 1951
CARSON CITY — Warner Bros. 1952
THE BIG TREES — Warner Bros. 1952
THE MISADVENTURES OF BUSTER KEATON — British Lion 1953
   [comprised of 1951 TV episodes; no U.S. theatrical release]
TAKE THE HIGH GROUND — MGM 1953
HIGHWAY DRAGNET — Allied Artists 1954
CRIME WAVE (The City Is Dark) — Warner Bros. 1954
THE FAST AND THE FURIOUS — American Releasing 1954
THE HELEN MORGAN STORY — Warner Bros. 1957
CARNIVAL ROCK — Howco International 1957
THE BUCCANEER — Paramount 1958
THE ERRAND BOY — Paramount 1961
BLUE HAWAII — Paramount 1961
FATE IS THE HUNTER — 20th Century-Fox 1964
THAT DARN CAT! — Disney-Buena Vista 1965
THE ODD COUPLE — Paramount 1968
THE LOVE BUG — Disney-Buena Vista 1969
THE BAREFOOT EXECUTIVE — Disney-Buena Vista 1971
SCANDALOUS JOHN — Disney-Buena Vista 1971
THE APPLE DUMPLING GANG — Disney-Buena Vista 1975
FREAKY FRIDAY — Disney-Buena Vista 1976
THE SHAGGY D.A. — Disney-Buena Vista 1976
GUS — Disney-Buena Vista 1976
NO DEPOSIT, NO RETURN — Disney-Buena Vista 1976
THE END — United Artists 1978 *scenes deleted*
GETTING MARRIED — Paramount-Moonlight-CBS 1978 [TV movie]
HERBIE GOES BANANAS — Disney-Buena Vista 1980
MURDER CAN HURT YOU! — Aaron Spelling-ABC 1980 [TV movie]
PATERNITY — Paramount 1981

Sam Jaffe

*I was awed by Sam Jaffe not only as an actor, but as a man. He was a
pillar of wisdom off screen as well as on. He could discuss virtually any
subject, be it art, music, politics or current events. Yet he was modest
and unpretentious; he delighted in telling stories about other people
but talked about himself with reluctance. He was a legend who made
little of his accomplishments — and a man who was perfectly comple-
mented by his gracious and devoted wife, Bettye.*

From the idealistic High Lama to the noble Gunga Din, to the
venerable Dr. Zorba, Sam Jaffe was hugely selective about the parts
he played. Few performers have his integrity: when Jaffe died in 1984,
he was eulogized as an actor who turned down more offers than most
actors ever accept.

"I only want to do a part that means something, that has something to say," Jaffe affirmed in an interview, a few years before his
death. "You can still watch *Lost Horizon* today, because it has
something to tell you. It was pure and inspirational," he said of the
1937 classic.

"*The Day The Earth Stood Still* had something to say: don't be so
proud of your atomic energy. I did other films that weren't so great,
but they were interesting — like *Under the Gun*, which was revealing
of the terrible treatment in prisons."

"I was the same in the theater. I always wanted a role that meant
something. There was a time when you went to the theater as
though you went to learn something about yourself — now it moves
into the bedroom," declared Jaffe. "The theater had something to tell
us in those days. It was entertainment, too, but it told you something
about yourself."

Jaffe was greatly admired and looked up to by the younger
members of the acting profession, many of whom he helped when
they were getting started. The Equity Library Theater — which he
founded with George Freedley in 1948 — is but part of his legacy; the
program, a subsidiary of Actor's Equity, has given thousands of
young performers their first exposure. Jaffe was also instrumental in
getting rehearsal pay for Equity actors.

"Sam was the kind of person I would like to become as I grow older
— not in terms of talent perhaps, but in the way that he helped

As Grand Duke Peter in *The Scarlet Empress* (1934).

people," says veteran actor and longtime friend Marvin Kaplan. "He knew how to help actors in a personal, immediate way. Sam was an ideal, an example for everybody.

"He was humble — you never got the the feeling he was an actor. He was a great artist. He could transform his body, voice and psyche into anybody he was playing; he was the consummate character actor. Whenever they needed somebody to play an Einstein-like character, someone of great intellect or spiritual quality, they always cast Sam."

Shalom Jaffe was born March 10, 1891 in New York City, the youngest of four children; "farmed out" by his mother, he was raised by his aunt. He could be vague when questioned about his age in later years. (Told that none of several sources agreed on his date of birth, Sam retorted, "I agree with none of the sources.")

Jaffe graduated from City College of New York with a B.S., intent on a career as a scientist and mathematician. He became a teacher, then dean of mathematics at the Bronx Cultural Institute, before turning his back on academia. "Somehow or other it goes along, you can't explain it... my mother, Ada Jaffe, was an actress in the Yiddish theater and I used to visit her at work," he recalled. "Shakespeare was a dominant force with me; it was inspirational. I felt I could express myself in the theater. "

"All actors have the potential of being great. It's a matter of opportunity."

As the High Lama, with Ronald Colman and Frank Capra on the set of *Lost Horizon* (1937).

He made his professional debut with the Washington Square Players in 1915. After touring with them as an understudy, he played the college circuit with Kearn's Sommes Shakespeare Company. Among Jaffe's early New York stage appearances were *To Be or Not To Be*, a vaudeville sketch which starred a young James Cagney (Sam directed and played his mother's husband); *Samson and Delilah* with Edward G. Robinson (they met at Townsend Harris High School); and *Ruint* with 17-year-old John Huston in the lead — long before Hollywood bestowed overnight success on any of them.

Robinson and Huston became lifelong friends of his, as a result of the bonds that developed in those early years. Sam also met his first wife, singer and musical comedy actress Lillian Taiz, in the early 1920s, when they did *The God of Vengeance* together at Province-town.

Beginning in 1925, he played Yudelson in *The Jazz Singer* for a three-year run, opposite George Jessel. They were on tour when the film version opened, forcing them to close. "Jessel and I were supposed to do the film, but George asked for more money than they wanted to pay," recalled Jaffe. "That canceled us both out."

Herman Shumlin's landmark production of *Grand Hotel* again brought Jaffe to the attention of movie producers. Louis B. Mayer saw the show and met the New York cast, but MGM decided to go with an all-star film version. Sam lost the role of Kringelein, the consumptive bookkeeper — his biggest stage success — to Lionel Barrymore.

Jaffe finally made his long-delayed screen debut in a powdered wig — opposite Marlene Dietrich — in Josef von Sternberg's *The Scarlet Empress*. Oddly enough, he won the part of the zany Grand Duke Peter as a result of his *Grand Hotel* screen test.

Sternberg dominated not only Dietrich but all aspects of the 1934 production, according to Jaffe. "He was a magnificent cameraman — he always rode the boom — but he was a strange man," said the actor. "He had a moustache, which I believe he painted on every day.

"I had to make a speech in *The Scarlet Empress* in which I was very much opposed to the queen, and Sternberg didn't like it. I did it about 38 times. Finally he said, 'If you don't do it well, the next time I'll have you go in and spit.' I said, 'If I spit, it will be right in your face,' and I took my wig off — the film hadn't been finished.

"Sternberg said, 'You'll never be able to work in films again.' I said, 'I don't want to be in films — you do.' He told me he had 70 million followers in Japan alone. I said, 'Strange, Christ only had 12.'"

Some 23 actors reportedly tested for the part of the High Lama — the 200-year-old priest who presides over the utopian paradise of Shangri-La — for Frank Capra's *Lost Horizon*. But Capra himself has stated that only two actors were actually tested: A.E. Anson, who died shortly after the test, and Jaffe.

"I had read the book and was inspired by it," Jaffe reflected. "This character was an idealist. He looked for a kind of world to which most people aspire — so you had to bring out whatever you had that was pure and idealistic. How the mind does it, I don't know; you use whatever you have within you.

"Capra was wonderful. The great thing about his direction, he looked into your eyes to make sure you knew what you were saying, that it boiled out of your own thought. He was marvelous in that respect. We spoke about the character but he didn't try to impose anything on you. That's the difference between Capra and Sternberg. A great director leaves you alone; he relies on you to bring about the character."

"Sam told me how he visualized the Lama," says Marvin Kaplan. "His body was made almost of glass, the hands were almost immobile.

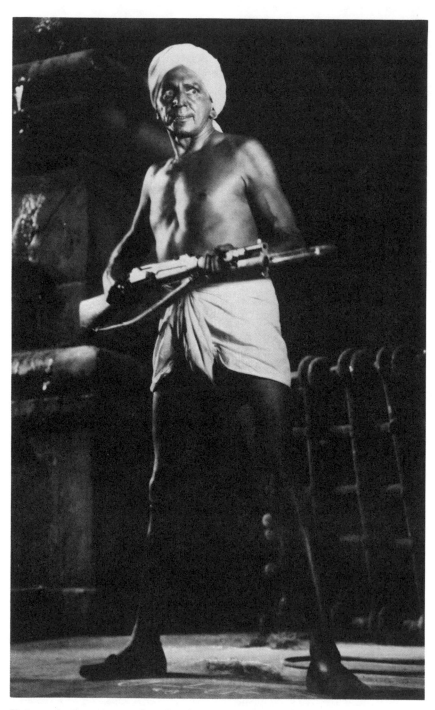

Fighting for the cause, in the title role of *Gunga Din* (1939).

All you could see through the glass was the spirit of the man's mind." (Ronald Colman wired Jaffe after seeing the film: "You completely stole the picture. As usual your performance surpasses all others.")

Following the film Jaffe did Max Reinhardt's *The Eternal Road* in New York, then went to Europe with Reinhardt. When he returned to the States, he was asked to redo his scenes for *Lost Horizon*, which had come out too dark. A horror story Jaffe revealed in later years — and Capra denied — was that the scenes were reshot with Walter Connolly in the five-month interim, because Columbia studio boss Harry Cohn "didn't want a Jew playing the Lama." Both versions of the film were previewed, with Sam declared the winner.

Jaffe recalled George Stevens, who put the actor through his paces in the title role of RKO's *Gunga Din* (1939), as "a kindly, able man, very bright. On the battlefield, he had to be a general — but he knew everything. I have only praise for him."

While he remembered Cary Grant, Victor McLaglen and Douglas Fairbanks Jr. as "wonderful people," Jaffe noted with amusement that his wife called the film "The Great Close-up" because "every time one of the stars would get a close-up, the others would phone their agent, that they should get the close-up too."

As Rudyard Kipling's "regimental beastie," who yearns to be a soldier — and is posthumously made a corporal — Sam drew on an unlikely inspiration. "I had seen Sabu in *Elephant Boy*, and I tried to emulate him, what I remembered from that one performance. I knew nothing about Hindus," he admitted. "I tried to approach the character a little bit in the dialect Sabu had. You must go back to a source occasionally, and this was a source for me." (Ironically, the popular young Indian actor had tested for the part himself.)

Jaffe made only the rare film appearance in the 1930s and '40s, such was his dedication to the stage. He agreed to do *Gunga Din* only with the provision that he would be free in time to play Shylock in the Penn State University production of *The Merchant of Venice*, to which he'd already committed.

Always willing to experiment, Jaffe took part in the 1939 Group Theatre production of *The Gentle People*. While the experience proved agreeable, he took exception to the company's Stanislavsky-inspired school of Method acting. "I found it interesting, the way they prepared for the play. But there is no Method. Everyone has his own way of approaching a part," he maintained. "Everything has to be organic; it has to spring from itself. Always there's a little mystery connected with it."

Two years later, he accepted the title role in *King Lear* at the New School — much to his regret. "The director had an idea — every-

As Dr. Riedenschneider, with Marc Lawrence in *The Asphalt Jungle* (1950).

thing had to tell a story. He had you repeat certain things; he wanted to be sure [the audience] didn't miss anything. That *Lear* was very unsatisfactory to me," said Sam, who was a purist when it came to Shakespeare. More to his liking was a less-trumpeted production of *The Kings' Maid* by Ferenc Molnar, who became a close friend.

When his first wife died in 1941, it was another pal, Zero Mostel — then a night club comic — who helped Sam over the loss. Night after night, the slightly-built Jaffe and the large, boisterous Mostel would stroll the avenues of Manhattan, looking for amusement; they often fed pigeons in Central Park at 3 a.m.

The actor scored a personal success when he returned to Broadway the following year as Hymie, a wise-cracking busboy, in *Cafe Crown*. (Hymie's real-life prototype, a waiter in New York's Cafe Royal, was so flattered he carried Sam's glowing notices around in his pocket.)

Jaffe was at the height of his career when his involvement in Actor's Equity — and other purportedly communist causes — resulted in his being blacklisted. His portrayal of Dr. Riedenschneider, the criminal mastermind of John Huston's *The Asphalt Jungle* (1950), had just won the Venice International award for Actor of the Year, and an Academy Award nomination for Best Supporting Actor.

"That McCarthy period was just terrible," said Jaffe, who claimed

As Dr. Zorba, with Bettye Ackerman on the set of *Ben Casey*.

he was "gray-listed" after *Gunga Din* (the FBI would follow him home after Equity meetings). While he wasn't bitter, he could be blunt when asked about it in later years: "Ronald Reagan was fingering people for Senator McCarthy," he told a documentary filmmaker.

Sam lost out on a number of film roles in the 1950s, due to the witchhunt. During this period he did Molnar's *The Blue Danube* on stage with Zero Mostel, another victim of the blacklist; he also toured in *Saint Joan* and played the title role in *Tartuffe* at the Ivar Theatre in Hollywood.

During a 1956 reprise of the Moliere farce in New York, he met his second wife, Bettye Ackerman. While he chased her on stage as well as off, he tried to dissuade the young actress from marrying him; he pointed out he was 37 years her senior, and insisted his future was behind him. Mostel was best man at their wedding. ("He called me Sam's child bride," says Bettye).

It was director Henri-Georges Clouzot who finally broke the blacklist, importing Jaffe to France for *Les Espions* (1957). Hollywood followed suit soon after, when John Huston hired him for *The Barbarian and the Geisha* and MGM cast him as Simonides in William Wyler's remake of *Ben Hur*.

Jaffe said no when Hollywood — and producer Howard Koch — asked him to play Dr. David Zorba in the pilot for ABC-TV's *Ben*

Casey. Though he had appeared on *Playhouse 90* and other programs, the fiercely independent actor had no desire to be tied down to a weekly television series. But he was courted relentlessly, until he finally agreed to play the hospital chief of staff.

While Jaffe was waiting for a costume fitting, his wife was asked to read for the role of Dr. Maggie Graham. To her surprise, Bettye ended up on the show alongside Sam and Vince Edwards; the actress who was to play the part had just been fired.

Despite an Emmy nomination for his performance during the first season (1961-62), Jaffe soon tired of the repetition. He stuck with it for four seasons, until he found a loophole in the contract. More recognizable than ever, he grew a full beard after leaving the series; he became so attached to it he turned down any role that required him to shave.

While Jaffe emerged from the blacklist with his integrity intact, his film career was never fully to recover. Unchallenged by the roles offered — and frequently offended by the scripts — he channeled his talents more often toward the small screen.

Arkady Leokum's *Enemies*, on public TV, gave Jaffe one of his meatiest parts in later years, as a crafty old waiter who engages in a battle of wits with a longtime customer. In *Gideon's Trumpet*, he played Supreme Court jurist Felix Frankfurter; he felt the latter role — for which he sacrificed his beard — was small but worthwhile.

"Stanislavsky said there are small actors, but no small parts. That isn't true. There are small parts and there are better parts. But there are no small actors," he demurred. "The actor who plays a small part one day may have the potential of being a big star; it's a matter of opportunity."

Unlike most actors, the size of the paycheck was never a consideration. "The money isn't the great thing. Money is in a sense a recognition of what you've done. How many pools can you have?" said Jaffe. "When Einstein was offered a position at Princeton, they asked him how much he wanted. He said, 'How much does one need to live?'"

Jaffe was sympathetic with those who could not afford to be as choosy as he was. "It's very tough to get started. You must be convinced that is what you want to do, and so you make sacrifices for it. Something takes you by the scruff of the neck and says, 'This is it,' and you stick to it," he conceded. "An actor is a man against the world."

The actor who so often played scholars and men of wisdom was, appropriately, a voracious reader — as well as a linguist and a composer. "An actor has to be aware of what's happening in the world,"

With Edward G. Robinson in *The Old Man Who Cried Wolf* (1970).

declared Jaffe. "We cannot know enough. Socrates said, 'Knowledge is power.' And it is. Your power grows as your knowledge grows. When you stop growing, you're dead."

Increasingly frail toward the end, Sam never stopped working. While he made his final stage appearance in the 1979 Broadway production of Christopher Isherwood's *A Meeting By the River* — as a Gandhi-like guru — he was by no means retired. Considering his fragile health, he was in fact remarkably busy in the last five years of his career — five movies, two documentaries and several TV appearances.

Among his last roles were that of a Strasberg-style drama coach in a film about Jayne Mansfield, and the ethereal Father Knickerbocker in the fantasy comedy, *Nothing Lasts Forever*. (Neither has been released). In 1983, Sam and Bettye did a *Love Boat* written especially for them; he also narrated *West of Hester Street*, an award-winning documentary about Texas Jews.

That fall, at 92, he played a smuggler of illegal aliens in the film *On the Line*. His scene was shot in an outdoor marketplace in the middle of the night; it was cold and wet, but neither illness nor inclement weather kept Jaffe from meeting his commitment.

John Huston planned to star his friend of nearly 60 years as the don of the Prizzi family in *Prizzi's Honor*, but it was not to be. On March 24, 1984, two weeks after his 93rd birthday, Jaffe succumbed to cancer at his Beverly Hills home.

Less than 48 hours before the end, the actor uttered a fitting epitaph in conversation with one of his nurses. "Sam," she said, "you're fantastic." "Yes," replied the patient. "Fantastic. Elastic. Iconoclastic."

The actor at his Beverly Hills home in 1980.

THE FILMS OF SAM JAFFE

Jaffe did not appear in ACE OF ACES (1933), ALL MINE TO GIVE (1957), or THE KREMLIN LETTER (1970) as recorded elsewhere. A number of TV specials and plays in which he did appear have been incorrectly listed as TV movies in certain references. Film clips of Jaffe were used in the documentary, GEORGE STEVENS: A FILMMAKER'S JOURNEY (1985). The title is unavailable for the documentary on the blacklist in which he appeared.

THE SCARLET EMPRESS — Paramount 1934
WE LIVE AGAIN — United Artists 1934
LOST HORIZON — Columbia 1937
GUNGA DIN — RKO 1939
STAGE DOOR CANTEEN — United Artists 1943
13 RUE MADELEINE — 20th Century-Fox 1946
GENTLEMAN'S AGREEMENT — 20th Century-Fox 1947
THE ACCUSED — Paramount 1949
ROPE OF SAND — Paramount 1949
THE ASPHALT JUNGLE — MGM 1950
UNDER THE GUN — Universal 1950
I CAN GET IT FOR YOU WHOLESALE — 20th Century-Fox 1951
THE DAY THE EARTH STOOD STILL — 20th Century-Fox 1951
LES ESPIONS — Filmsonor 1957
THE BARBARIAN AND THE GEISHA — 20th Century-Fox 1958
BEN HUR — MGM 1959
A GUIDE FOR THE MARRIED MAN — 20th Century-Fox 1967
GUNS FOR SAN SEBASTIAN — MGM 1968
THE GREAT BANK ROBBERY — Warner Bros. Seven Arts 1969
NIGHT GALLERY — Universal-NBC 1969 [TV movie]
THE DUNWICH HORROR — American International Pictures 1970
QUARANTINED (House on the Hill) — Paramount-ABC 1970 [TV movie]
THE OLD MAN WHO CRIED WOLF — ABC 1970 [TV movie]
TARZAN'S JUNGLE REBELLION — National General 1970 [comprised of
    TV episodes; no U.S. theatrical release]
BEDKNOBS AND BROOMSTICKS — Disney-Buena Vista 1971
SAM HILL: WHO KILLED THE MYSTERIOUS MR. FOSTER? — Universal-
    NBC 1971 [TV movie]
THE TELL-TALE HEART — American Film Institute 1971 [short]
NEXT YEAR IN JERUSALEM — CBC 1974 [documentary]
QB VII — Screen Gems-Columbia-ABC 1974 [TV movie]
THE END — United Artists 1978 *scenes deleted*
BATTLE BEYOND THE STARS — New World 1980
GIDEON'S TRUMPET — Gideon Productions-CBS 1980 [TV movie]
JAYNE MANSFIELD — AN AMERICAN TRAGEDY — Starmar Productions
    1980 (The Jayne Mansfield Story) [no theatrical release]
NOTHING LASTS FOREVER — MGM 1982 [no theatrical release]
WEST OF HESTER STREET — Media Projects 1983 [documentary]
    narrator
ON THE LINE (Downstream, Rio Abajo) — Amber Films 1984 [no U.S.
    theatrical release]

Beulah Bondi

Beulah Bondi turned down my first request for an interview. Years later, she granted me an audience at her home in the Hollywood Hills — just two months before she died. I was met not by the elderly grandmother type I half expected, but a woman with an outlook on life that belied her years. She wore old age with dignity and youth; there was a radiance in her face undimmed by time and a presence as vivid as any of her screen characters.

At the outset of her distinguished career, Beulah Bondi was taken to task by a director for being "too soft." If she failed to appreciate the criticism in 1919, she later realized her freshman year in Stuart Walker's stock company made all the difference.

"Mr. Walker was very severe that first summer in Indianapolis," the actress recalled, in her last interview. "He told me years later, he knew I had talent, and that the theater was a hard life. He was either going to make me or break me; he was very hard on me, but would always give me a pat on the back when I did things right.

"That dressing down from Mr. Walker helped prepare me for a life in the theater," asserted Bondi. "He put a good tough hide on me so I could not be hurt or disappointed. By his preparing me, I never have felt in any way timid or apprehensive when I meet a new producer or director. I can meet them on an equal footing."

From her career breakthrough in *Street Scene* a decade later, to her eloquent portrayals in such films as *Make Way for Tomorrow* and *Of Human Hearts*, Bondi rarely misjudged her footing. Her reputation as Hollywood's preeminent character actress remains unchallenged, in death as in life, with no apparent successor on the horizon.

Born in Chicago on May 3, 1888 (not 1892, as often recorded), Beulah Bondy made her professional debut at the age of 7, as Cedric Erroll in *Little Lord Fauntleroy*. She changed the spelling of her last name in an attempt to pacify family members who disapproved.

"My mother encouraged me from an early age — as soon as I could walk," said Bondi. "She seemed to think that was my talent, and that was what she had to give. I could remember lines easily. I don't remember the first time I performed, because I was probably three or four."

"Beulah Bondi is completely hidden in the parts I've played."

Her father was one of those who disapproved. "As an adolescent, I recall going to a play with my parents, and there was a very fine actor, Grant Mitchell, in the show. Afterwards I said to my father, 'Surely you wouldn't object if I got into a company with such a fine gentleman.' My father said, 'He's playing a gentleman — we don't know if he is one.'" Her father lived to see her success, and give her his blessing.

Bondi received her early training at the Chicago Little Theatre — where she studied dance and diction — under the guidance of Maurice Browne. She graduated from Frances Shimer Academy (now Shimer College) and earned a master's degree in oratory from Valparaiso University before joining the Stuart Walker Stock Company.

One fortuitous day in 1927, with one off-Broadway play to her credit (*Wild Birds*), she bumped into Melville Burke — one of Walker's directors — while job-hunting in New York. "He said, 'Come with me. I'm starting rehearsal on a new play, and they need an old lady — I know you can do it and I'll fight your battles for you.' The character was about 80 years old."

Within weeks of opening in *One of the Family*, she began rehears als for Guthrie McClintic's production of *Saturday's Children*. While playing the role of an unpleasant, tight-lipped landlady — opposite Ruth Gordon — in the latter, McClintic put her in another show opening in the theater next door.

"I think that was the first time an actress did two plays at the same time," said Bondi, who found herself playing a choir singer — "a very pleasant woman" — in the first act of *Mariners*, then changing her makeup and going next door for the last act of *Saturday's Children*. McClintic subsequently cast her in *Cock Robin* and *Distant Drums*.

Elmer Rice's *Street Scene* — which opened at the Playhouse Theatre in January 1929, and ran for 601 performances on Broadway — finally brought the actress to prominence in the role of Emma Jones, the malicious neighborhood gossip. But she was so cocky she almost lost out.

"Mr. Rice had written the part for me," she recalled. "I was already in rehearsal for another play when he called. He said, 'You can get out of it.' I took his play home and read it; it was wonderful.

"William Brady was producing it. He was known to be very tough; actors didn't like him. He offered me $75 a week for the show. I said, 'Frankly, Mr. Brady, when I first came to New York I got $175.' He said, 'If you think you can get a job at $175 a week, you take it.' I said, 'If you think you can get an actress of my standing for $75 a week, get her.'

With director Clarence Brown on the set of *The Gorgeous Hussy* (1936).

"I explained to Mr. Rice that I was getting $275 for the show I was rehearsing to be in. He said, 'I'll see what I can do.' He wanted me for the role, and I wanted to do it; it was a much better play. They came to me and said, 'What would you think of taking $375, plus a percentage of the show?'" remembered Bondi, savoring her triumph. "Of course, the show was an instantaneous success."

Bondi began her film career when King Vidor brought her to Hollywood to recreate her role in the 1931 screen version. Her performance was hailed by the critics, but when Sam Goldwyn and Irving Thalberg offered her a seven-year contract as a result — guarantying Bondi $500 a week — she tore it up.

Among Bondi's earliest films were *Arrowsmith*, *Rain* and *Stranger's Return*. The latter found her working with Lionel Barrymore for the first time. "He was on drugs then. He was very ill," she recalled. "He was rather difficult. He said, 'Don't pay any attention to me. I'm just an old so-and-so.' He was using all sorts of foul language. I told him to behave himself, and we got along fine."

Bondi did several films with Barrymore, and also appeared on his radio show, *Mayor of the Town*. When they worked together on *Christopher Bean* — in which she repeated her stage role as a nagging wife — Bondi had still more trouble with her co-star.

"There was a good laugh on one line, and every time I was about to do the line he'd pass his hand across my face. We did it twice, then they said, 'We'll take one more for insurance.' I grabbed his wrist and squeezed it tight and said my line. He looked at me and he said, 'I'll be good.' He put people to the test to see how much they knew. I never had any difficulty with him after that.

"Working with the different stars, I've enjoyed each and every one, and have always had this great empathy and feeling for them. But I couldn't socialize with them," the actress explained. "Between scenes, I have to be by myself. That way the character stays with me.

"I knew the stars as the characters they played. I played Jimmy Stewart's mother five times. I didn't feel like he was Jimmy Stewart — he was my son. And they were all different sons." Bondi, to her credit, played five very different mothers to Stewart's sons, beginning with *The Gorgeous Hussy* in 1936 (as Mrs. Andrew Johnson), and concluding with a 1971 episode of the actor's NBC-TV series.

"No two characters are alike," Bondi maintained. "Every one has their own personality. I've always felt that a character was the result of all her yesterdays. I take her from the start, as a young girl. What was her life? What were her experiences, her thoughts, her actions?

"If she was an unpleasant character, for instance, maybe she had a drunken husband — or ungrateful children. Every character ever given to me was a different individual; none of them were alike, so they were all a challenge. One thing I've always tried to do was hide my own personality. Beulah Bondi is completely hidden in the parts I've played."

One thing that always amused Bondi was buying clothes for her characters. For *Street Scene*, she bought a dress that was much too big. "The sales lady pulled it together in back when I looked in the mirror, and when I turned around to look in back, she gathered it in the front. She said, 'It looks very nice on you.' It shows how dishonest sales people can be," she noted with amusement.

Leo McCarey's *Make Way for Tomorrow* (1937) — in which she and Victor Moore play an elderly couple trying to retain some dignity in their last years — was once cited by Bondi as her favorite film. Later she claimed she had no preferences. "That film seems to be a favorite now," she acknowledged, "but it wasn't a success when it came out. People said, 'We don't need to see somebody else's troubles.'"

In contrast to the hundreds of wives and mothers she portrayed, in a career that spanned six decades, the actress never married. "I've never regretted the choice of a career over marriage. It was a difficult decision," she admitted, "but the career won out. And I've never been sorry."

Bondi, who felt that much of her life was coincidence — "being in the right place at the right time" — had but two disappointments in her career. Curiously enough, they were engineered by two of Hollywood's legendary moguls — David Selznick and Darryl Zanuck.

She had been warned about Selznick when first asked to play Aunt Polly in *The Adventures of Tom Sawyer*. He had started production in black and white, filmed for a month, then fired everyone and started over in color — according to a friend of hers. "Don't be surprised if he fires you," Bondi was told. Sure enough, she worked on the picture for a month before she was dropped and replaced by May Robson.

With Victor Moore in *Make Way for Tommorrow* (1937).

She never found out why.

Losing out on the plum role of Ma Joad in *The Grapes of Wrath* was an ever greater disappointment. "I was told I was the only one being considered. They lied to me," she said. "I went up to Bakersfield [Central California] and visited and talked with migrant workers. I went to five different Okie camps. I dressed in old clothes; no one recognized me.

"I wasn't up there long, but I was all prepared to do the film; I'd gotten acquainted with many different types of women. When I came back I did two tests. The man playing my husband in the tests spilled the beans. He said, 'I'm just an extra, but of the five actresses I've played opposite against in this part, you're the best.'

"John Ford was very pleased with the tests. But Mr. Zanuck said I was not the type. They ended up casting Jane Darwell. She was a fine actress — no jealousy there — but the thing was, they lied to me,"

With Lionel Barrymore in *On Borrowed Time* (1939).

In costume for *She's a Soldier Too* (1944).

asserted Bondi. "Ford even said I was the best one for the role. But Darwell was a contract player, so there was a big difference in our salaries. I don't think Ma Joad should've been so portly, so well fed," she observed. "There were no big women [like Darwell] among the women at the camps."

Darwell won an Academy Award for Best Supporting Actress in the role. Bondi, who garnered two nominations (for *The Gorgeous Hussy* and *Of Human Hearts*) but never won an Oscar, emerged from the experience with a typically sunny attitude: "It was great preparation, which I've never regretted."

Despite her success in films, Bondi never deserted the stage. In 1950, she returned to Broadway to appear in *Hilda Crane*, with Jessica Tandy; three years later, she was back, recreating her *film* role in *On Borrowed Time* opposite Victor Moore. She also did the latter play in Los Angeles, with Boris Karloff as her co-star.

While her film roles diminished in the 1950s (a mere nine pictures, compared to 25 the previous decade), Bondi was often called for television work. She appeared on such early programs as *Goodyear Playhouse*, *G.E. Theatre*, *Climax* and *Alfred Hitchcock Presents*.

In her eighties, she found worthwhile roles few and far between (suitable movie work, following *Tammy and the Doctor* in 1963, proved nonexistent). A stand out among her later TV appearances was *Sandburg's Lincoln: Crossing Fox River*, opposite Hal Holbrook. Her portrayal of Aunt Martha on "The Pony Cart" episode of *The Waltons* late in 1976 won her an Emmy, as Best Actress in a single appearance. It was, appropriately, her final dramatic role.

On January 2, 1981, the 92-year-old actress fell and broke her ribs in her Spanish-style home in Hollywood's Whitley Heights neighborhood, where she had lived alone for nearly 40 years. Bondi was admitted to the Motion Picture Country Hospital, where she died January 11, after pulmonary complications set in.

To the end, Bondi was enchanted with life. She never tired of traveling to new places — she went on a two-month long safari in Africa when she was 83 — or meeting new challenges. "People keep asking if I've retired," she said shortly before her death. "No, I haven't. But I don't get offered many parts today. Last year [1979] I was offered a film but I didn't like the language in it." To her chagrin, when the picture came out Bondi discovered, "there wasn't a word in it I couldn't have said — and it was a big success."

The actress at her Hollywood home in 1980.

THE FILMS OF BEULAH BONDI

Some TV specials in which Bondi appeared, such as TOMORROW (1960) and SANDBURG'S LINCOLN: CROSSING FOX RIVER (1976), have been erroneously listed as TV movies in certain references.

STREET SCENE — Goldwyn-United Artists 1931
ARROWSMITH — Goldwyn-United Artists 1931
RAIN — United Artists 1932
STRANGER'S RETURN — MGM 1933
CHRISTOPHER BEAN (Her Sweetheart) — MGM 1933
TWO ALONE — RKO Radio 1934
FINISHING SCHOOL — RKO Radio 1934
REGISTERED NURSE — First National 1934
READY FOR LOVE — Paramount 1934
THE PAINTED VEIL — MGM 1934   *scenes reshot with Bodil Rosing*
BAD BOY — Fox 1935
THE GOOD FAIRY — Universal 1935
TRAIL OF THE LONESOME PINE — Paramount 1936
THE INVISIBLE RAY — Universal 1936
THE MOON'S OUR HOME — Paramount 1936
THE CASE AGAINST MRS. AMES — Paramount 1936
HEARTS DIVIDED — First National 1936
THE GORGEOUS HUSSY — MGM 1936
MAID OF SALEM — Paramount 1937
MAKE WAY FOR TOMORROW — Paramount 1937
THE BUCCANEER — Paramount 1938
VIVACIOUS LADY — RKO Radio 1938
OF HUMAN HEARTS — MGM 1938
THE SISTERS — Warner Bros. 1938
THE ADVENTURES OF TOM SAWYER — United Artists 1938
    scenes reshot with May Robson
ON BORROWED TIME — MGM 1939
MR. SMITH GOES TO WASHINGTON — Columbia 1939
THE UNDER-PUP — Universal 1939
OUR TOWN — United Artists 1940
THE CAPTAIN IS A LADY — MGM 1940
REMEMBER THE NIGHT — Paramount 1940
PENNY SERENADE — Columbia 1941
SHEPHERD OF THE HILLS — Paramount 1941
ONE FOOT IN HEAVEN — Warner Bros. 1941
WATCH ON THE RHINE — Warner Bros. 1943
TONIGHT WE RAID CALAIS — 20th Century-Fox 1943
I LOVE A SOLDIER — Paramount 1944
SHE'S A SOLDIER TOO — Columbia 1944

With Guy Kibbee (left) and Walter Huston in *Of Human Hearts* (1938).

AND NOW TOMORROW — Paramount 1944
THE VERY THOUGHT OF YOU — Warner Bros. 1944
OUR HEARTS WERE YOUNG AND GAY — Paramount 1944
BACK TO BATAAN — RKO Radio 1945
THE SOUTHERNER — United Artists 1945
BREAKFAST IN HOLLYWOOD — United Artists 1946
SISTER KENNY — RKO Radio 1946
IT'S A WONDERFUL LIFE — Liberty Films-RKO Radio 1946
HIGH CONQUEST — Monogram 1947
THE SAINTED SISTERS — Paramount 1948
THE SNAKE PIT — 20th Century-Fox 1948
SO DEAR TO MY HEART — Disney-RKO Radio 1948
THE LIFE OF RILEY — Universal-International 1949
MR. SOFT TOUCH (House of Settlement) — Columbia 1949
REIGN OF TERROR (The Black Book) — Eagle-Lion 1949

With Diana Dors in *The Unholy Wife* (1957).

THE BARON OF ARIZONA — Lippert Pictures 1950
THE FURIES — Paramount 1950
LONE STAR — MGM 1952
LATIN LOVERS — MGM 1953
TRACK OF THE CAT — Warner Bros. 1954
BACK FROM ETERNITY — RKO Radio 1956
THE UNHOLY WIFE — Universal 1957
THE BIG FISHERMAN — Centurion Films-Buena Vista 1959
A SUMMER PLACE — Warner Bros. 1959
TAMMY TELL ME TRUE — Universal-International 1961
THE WONDERFUL WORLD OF THE BROTHERS GRIMM —
    MGM-Cinerama 1962
TAMMY AND THE DOCTOR — Universal-International 1963
SHE WAITS — Metromedia-CBS 1972 [TV movie]

Fritz Feld

Fritz Feld is as eccentric — and as energetic — in real life as he is on screen. He has more has more stamina than most people I know; he may be 50 years my senior, but I find myself exhausted after spending the better part of a day with him. The welcome mat is always out at his hilltop home, and no visit is complete without an improvisational performance at the piano. His wife, Virginia, is as gracious as she is charming, and — all kidding aside — she makes a terrific cup of coffee.

When a movie producer needs a waiter or a maitre d', more often than not he calls on Fritz Feld. Hollywood is full of attention-getters, but few are more distinguished than the silver-haired, mustachioed actor, who finds his services much in demand as he approaches 86. In a career that spans seven decades, the German-born entertainer estimates he has made over 2,000 appearances on stage, screen, radio and television.

"The reason I've played so many parts is because producers could trust me not to steal scenes," contends Feld. "If there's a weak leading lady and a weak leading man, and I'm powerful, they disappear. So I underplay it. When I play a butler or a servant, the reason the audience likes me is because I'm the underdog; I don't take away from the leading man."

Acknowledging the fact that few stars remain from the great days of Hollywood, Feld asserts, "As a character actor you last longer. We don't have to worry about our appearance. Each studio had a different way of typing me: at Universal, I played only butlers; at Paramount, mostly counts with monocles; at MGM, conductors of symphony orchestras; at RKO, gamblers and strange individuals; at Fox, train conductors, postmen and ministers. Over and over I played the same parts. Then came hotel clerks, and then waiters. Then every studio wanted me to play a waiter or a maitre d'."

Despite the number of times he has donned that guise (*Barefoot in the Park*, *Hello, Dolly!*, etc.), Feld invests each role with something unique. "It doesn't bother me at all, playing so many waiters," he says. "Each one is different a little bit. What is the art of acting but observation? When I play a waiter it's not only the one I play but the many waiters I observe. How do they look to get their tip? How do they smile? How do they walk? I never mind how small a part is, the

71

The youthful protégé of Max Reinhardt.

fun is to make something out of it."

Fritz was playing a waiter in a 1948 Eddie Cantor picture (*If You Knew Susie*), when he found he could imitate the pop of a champagne cork by slapping his hand across his mouth — a trick which has since become his trademark. "My first trademark was clicking my heels, which I ended when a little boy put a nut between my feet," he recalls. "I clicked my heels and he said, 'Thank you, sir.' Then something else had to come, and it became the pop.

"It is wonderful if you go to god-forsaken places like New Guinea and American tourists recognize you from far away," enthuses the actor. "They say, 'For heaven's sake, do the pop for us!' In Africa I did the pop for one of the chiefs of the Masai tribe; he wanted to imitate me and he did it to perfection. It's interesting that a gimmick like this becomes so important and people remember you by it."

Fritz Feilchenfeld (translation: "field of violets") was born in Berlin, October 15, 1900, to a family devoted to art and music. As a youth he staged plays in a puppet theater built by his father; his older brother, Rudi, who was to become chief art director at Ufa, designed the sets. "That started us off," says Feld. "A cousin played small parts with Max Reinhardt, and she would tell me about it; I became theater-struck."

The aspiring young actor made his debut as an unpaid extra in a production of *William Tell* at Berlin's Royal Theater, circa 1916. While in high school he applied to Reinhardt's theater school, but was rejected. "They said, 'He will never become an actor because he lisps.' My father, who was a printer, said, 'That's it. Now you start in my business.' It didn't last long," says Feld. "I secretly went back to the school and passed the test. I spent two years there and became the master pupil; later I became Reinhardt's first assistant."

When Morris Gest asked Reinhardt to produce *The Miracle* in the United States, Fritz asked if he could go along. "Reinhardt said no," recounted Feld. "He said, 'I'm doing a holy play; I cannot take you. You are with the girls morning, noon and night. You will make trouble and the holy play will be no good.'" The musical director, however, liked Feld and wangled him a contract, to assist Reinhardt in staging the popular religious spectacle. Fate stepped in when the star, Werner Krauss, broke his leg; Fritz took over the leading role of The Piper, touring America with the show for over three years, beginning in 1923.

The young actor, who made his film debut in his native Germany (he was the court jester in the 1920 version of *Der Golem*), settled in Los Angeles shortly after *The Miracle* closed. Before long, he was signed for a featured role in *The Dove*, opposite Norma Talmadge.

"I worked for many months on this picture," he recalls. "There was a tremendous opening night at Grauman's Chinese and I invited a lot of friends. My scene came up but I didn't come on; I figured they probably cut it differently. I waited and waited and finally Talmadge turned to her lover and pointed — I was the one who made the lover jealous. There was a very far long shot; I stood and picked my teeth with a knife, and that was it. I was almost completely cut out of the picture. From that moment on I never invited anyone to an opening night."

Fritz was next cast as a grotesque Russian peddler in *The Tempest* with John Barrymore — an assignment that added insult to injury. At the request of director Slav Tourjansky, he grew a beard for the part. "He said, 'I want you to look syphilitic.' They cut pieces out of my beard left and right," says Feld. "I looked horrible. After making at least 14 different tests, one day the casting director said, 'I have sad news; the character has been cut out of the picture.'" Heartbroken, he later visited the set, only to discover a bearded man playing his role — "Tourjansky's best friend, from Russia." (Barrymore ended up firing both the director and the friend).

Broke and out of work, Feld went to Josef von Sternberg and begged him for a job. The director obliged, writing a part for him as a Russian revolutionist in *The Last Command* (1928), starring Emil Jannings. Feld still remembers the night when the director was having trouble with a crowd scene — and the star called him into his dressing room.

"I had worked with Jannings on the stage. He said, 'I know you were the first assistant of Max Reinhardt and directed all the mass scenes. How would you like to take over for Mr. Sternberg, that son of a bitch, and direct the picture?'

"I practically shit in my pants," says Feld. "Here comes the biggest star, and he asks me — all my life I've wanted to direct. I started thinking. I said, 'Mr. Jannings, I am honored, but I can't do it. I was broke and I asked Mr. Sternberg to give me a job. It would be a stab in his back to suddenly take over. What I can do is direct the masses, if you'll call him, and allow me to do it without credit.' That was arranged, and I did it. The great Sternberg was never able to direct the masses."

After acting in several silent and early sound films, Feld made it known that he wanted to direct. He began by directing a talking sequence in *The Godless Girl* for Cecil B. De Mille — "finding out later than no one would dare to do such a thing," he concedes. Fritz then turned his talents to the New York stage, where he directed Sydney

With Greta Grandstedt in *The Sorcerer's Apprentice* (1928).

Greenstreet in *Berlin* and helped stage the more successful *Grand Hotel*. He also worked as a dialog director on many films.

In 1934, Feld was named production chief for the Orient Film Corporation. While in the post he was assigned to direct the first all-Hebrew talking picture, *A New Life*, on location in Palestine and Syria; the project, however, was aborted in mid-production. He subsequently became editorial assistant to Ernst Lubitsch, who was then production chief at Paramount Pictures.

"I promised Lubitsch never to act again, because I wanted to direct," states Feld. "Hundreds of scripts went through me, then I would report to Lubitsch. He had a tremendous story mind. Before I could finish a story he would tell me the ending — and he was always right." Before Fritz had a chance to direct at Paramount, Lubitsch departed — first recommending his assistant to director Wesley Ruggles for the role of an indignant Swiss hotel clerk in *I Met Him in Paris* (1937).

As a result of that performance, Feld has found constant employment as an actor ever since. During the filming, he went to five of the biggest agencies in Hollywood seeking representation; they all rejected him. "After the picture came out, all the same agents came

With Katharine Hepburn in a scene cut from *Bringing Up Baby* (1938).

running — 'we want you.' I said, 'To hell with you; I'll get my own agent.'"

Before he found himself typecast at the various studios, Feld shaved his head to play a German soldier in Gregory Ratoff's *Lancer Spy*. He recalls it as one of his favorite parts, because "I got even with the Prussian Germans whom I didn't like, by playing an orderly. The master speaks — they jump."

Feld also found his Russian-born director — himself a prominent character actor — a most colorful individual. "Ratoff made a pact with me," reveals Feld. "He said 'Fritz, I'll tell you what I want you to do. I want fall guy. I want man whom I can bore the shit out of — and you're it. Now you don't talk back to me and I will be *horrid* to you. But I love you.' I made many pictures with him."

Another director he remembers fondly is Howard Hawks, who cast him as a flustered psychiatrist in the now-classic screwball comedy, *Bringing Up Baby* (1938). "One of the best written scenes in any picture was the one between Katharine Hepburn and I," says Feld. "She sits in the chair and I start to psychoanalyze her; it ends up

With Clark Gable and Norma Shearer in *Idiot's Delight* (1939).

that I sit and she psychoanalyzes me. The scene was cut out; it was the introduction of my character.

"Hawks invented for this film talking without cues; it was the first picture where actors talked at the same time, the way we talk in life." The director also had unusual working methods: "He would come in in the morning and say, 'I don't feel like working today. Let's go to the racetrack.' We went to the racetrack for two days, and he paid for everything."

Anatole Litvak, who directed the actor in *Tovarich*, was a real perfectionist — or so he thought. "He did 36 takes on one scene," recalls Feld. "He said, 'Print all 36.' The front office fixed him; they printed take one 36 times. He saw the rushes, he said, 'Take seven.' They said, 'That's take one.'"

Jerry Lewis, who cast Feld in a number of films, is "a very charming man," says the actor, "but he can turn like a chameleon into a very sadistic person. In one picture he made me do a dance step; I'm no dancer but I did what I could. He kept making me do it again and again: 'Goddamn it, do it right.' I said nothing and kept on doing it. I enjoyed it, because I looked through him; he's showing off some-times."

Of actors who have influenced him, Fritz notes, "I learned a lot from Edward Everett Horton. I imitate him many times, in my way of acting. I like the way he did things. Franklin Pangborn, Horton and I were the only actors in Hollywood that producers could trust — we never went overboard," says Feld. "It's different today; they play gays too grotesque. At that time you had to be careful."

Over the decades, the durable character actor has appeared as the conductor of a floating orchestra in the Marx Brothers' *At the Circus*; Lou Costello's prissy elocution teacher in *Mexican Hayride*; a beauty consultant in Frank Capra's *Pocketful of Miracles*; the gourmet food salesman who feeds chocolate-covered ants to Jerry Lewis in *Who's Minding the Store*; and an actor auditioning for a potato chip commercial in *The Sunshine Boys*.

He now finds himself revered by filmmakers like Mel Brooks, who gave him a title card that said "Pop!" in *Silent Movie* and later cast him as the maitre d' at The Last Supper in *History of the World — Part I*. Gene Wilder, an unabashed fan, featured Feld as the hotel manager in *The World's Greatest Lover* — a performance so broad it bordered on self-parody.

"When you search for the roots of movie comedy, the belly laughs of comedy, the people who were part of that are not so easy to find any more. Fritz Feld was part of that," says Wilder. "Each day I directed him was a great privilege. For me, working with Fritz was what comedy was all about."

Over the years, claims Feld, "comedy has not changed at all. The trouble is, the comedians have changed. Stand-up comics leave me cold; there's no class, no timing. Audiences have changed too. They think by being gross — saying dirty words — it's better. In a Lubitsch film, the light went out in the bedroom and we knew what was happening. We don't have to see. Guessing is the most beautiful thing, because imagination is at work.

"Brooks and Wilder deserve credit for bringing back comedy, but even they go overboard. It becomes a new trend — other people imitate them, and they go further overboard. Brooks does unbe-lievable gags, but his direction is entirely different from Lubitsch or Hawks," says Feld.

"I played a psychiatrist in a Lubitsch film with Merle Oberon [*That Uncertain Feeling*]. I say, 'What's your age?' She gives the age. I look up, I say, 'I'm your psychiatrist.' She changes immediately the age. Lubitsch says, 'No, no, Fritz, don't do that.' I ask her age. She says, '22.' I say, 'I'm your psychiatrist,' without looking up. She says, '26.' That's the Lubitsch touch."

In 1981, Fritz returned to the stage for the first time in over a decade, as Kolenkhov in a Los Angeles production of *You Can't Take It With You.* "I wanted to see if I could still get an audience," he notes. (He got standing ovations every night.)

"I think I'm the only actor who comes from the theater, who likes motion pictures better," says Feld. "Not to undermine what the stage can be, but I think it's more interesting to go from one picture to another. Television is not as challenging as film from an artistic standpoint; it's challenging because you have to work like a dog and do it in a short time."

Among his many TV appearances, Feld has been seen on *The Red Skelton Show, Lost in Space, Batman,* and *Love, American Style.* During the 1985-86 season he appeared on *Simon and Simon, Magnum, P.I.* and *Amazing Stories.* A longtime member of the Screen Actors Guild board of directors, he is also coordinator of the Fritz Feld Community Theater in Brentwood, California.

In the fall of 1985 the actor celebrated 45 years of marriage to actress Virginia Christine (nee Kraft), who was a singer when they met. "She wanted to be a dramatic actress," says Feld. "I told her she couldn't do both." Virginia made her debut in a stage production of *Hedda Gabler,* under the direction of her husband. Despite roles in such films as *High Noon* and *Guess Who's Coming to Dinner?* she is best known for her 21-year stint as Mrs. Olson in a series of TV coffee commercials.

While Feld's pace is unslowed by age, he feels he was "more daring" as a young man. "When you're older, you have more security, more confidence. You have a feeling nothing can happen to you — to hell with everything." Fritz, who is writing his autobiography (*Putting on the Fritz*), has but one regret: "I have a feeling I'm a much better director than actor. If I ever come to this world again, I'll be a director. But I'm a very lucky man," he asserts. "Look who I'm married to — she's a fool but I'm a lucky man."

As the hotel manager in *The World's Greatest Lover* (1977).

THE FILMS OF FRITZ FELD

Titles are unavailable for a number of silent films Feld made in Germany, including a short subject he also directed; he was an assistant to the director on WILHELM TELL (1923). He directed a talking sequence for THE GODLESS GIRL (1929) and also directed the aborted film, A NEW LIFE (1934). Feld was a dialog director on BEHIND THE MAKE-UP (1930), NIGHT ANGEL (1931), AND SUDDEN DEATH (1936) and other Paramount films before renewing his acting career. He did not appear in DER GOLEM UND DIE TÄNZERIN (1917), THE CHARLATAN (1929), FOUR JILLS IN A JEEP (1944), or JALOPY (1953), as recorded elsewhere. Based on a list compiled by Feld, and other sources.

Shorts

THE SORCERER'S APPRENTICE (The Wizard's Apprentice) —
    United Artists 1928
OUT WHERE THE STARS BEGIN — Warner Bros. 1938
SWINGTIME IN THE MOVIES — Warner Bros. 1939
QUIET PLEASE — Warner Bros. 1939
CUPID GOES NUTS — Columbia 1947
SO YOU WANT TO BE A DOCTOR — Warner Bros. 1951 [unreleased?]
SO YOU WANT TO ENJOY LIFE — Warner Bros. 1952
SO YOU WANT TO BE A MUSICIAN — Warner Bros. 1953
SO YOU WANT TO BE PRETTY — Warner Bros. 1956
FABRICS OF A DREAM — Fortrel 1962 [industrial]
MERCURY — Producers Studios 1963 [industrial]
THE MIRACLE — UCLA 1963 [student film]

Features

DER GOLEM: WIE ER IN DIE WELT KAM (The Golem: How He Came
    Into the World) — Ufa 1920
DÄMON DER WELT (Demon of the World) — Kahn Film 1920
CHRISTIAN WAHNSCHAFFE (The World's Illusion) — Terrafilm 1921
THE SWAN — Paramount 1925
THE DOVE — United Artists 1928
THE TEMPEST — United Artists 1928 scenes reshot with Boris De Fas
THE LAST COMMAND — Paramount 1928
A SHIP COMES IN (His Country) — Pathé 1928
BLINDFOLD — Fox 1928
THE LEOPARD LADY — Pathé 1928
ONE HYSTERICAL NIGHT (No, No Napoleon) — Universal 1929
BLACK MAGIC — Fox 1929
BROADWAY — Universal 1929
I MET HIM IN PARIS — Paramount 1937

EXPENSIVE HUSBANDS — Warner Bros. 1937
TRUE CONFESSION — Paramount 1937
LANCER SPY — 20th Century-Fox 1937
TOVARICH — Warner Bros. 1937
HOLLYWOOD HOTEL — Warner Bros. 1937
GO CHASE YOURSELF — RKO Radio 1938
AFFAIRS OF ANNABEL — RKO Radio 1938
BRINGING UP BABY — RKO Radio 1938
ROMANCE IN THE DARK — Paramount 1938
GOLD DIGGERS IN PARIS — Warner Bros. 1938
ARTISTS AND MODELS ABROAD — Paramount 1938
CAMPUS CONFESSIONS — Paramount 1938
I'LL GIVE A MILLION — 20th Century-Fox 1938
IDIOT'S DELIGHT — MGM 1939
AT THE CIRCUS — MGM 1939
LITTLE ACCIDENT — Universal 1939
WHEN TOMORROW COMES — Universal 1939
EVERYTHING HAPPENS AT NIGHT — 20th Century-Fox 1939
LITTLE OLD NEW YORK — 20th Century-Fox 1940
IT'S A DATE — Universal 1940
MA! HE'S MAKING EYES AT ME — Universal 1940
MILLIONAIRE PLAYBOY — RKO Radio 1940
I WAS AN ADVERTURESS — 20th Century-Fox 1940
SANDY IS A LADY — Universal 1940
VICTORY — Paramount 1940
COME LIVE WITH ME — MGM 1941
WORLD PREMIERE — Paramount 1941
YOU BELONG TO ME — Columbia 1941
MEXICAN SPITFIRE'S BABY — RKO Radio 1941
SKYLARK — Paramount 1941
THREE SONS O' GUNS — Warner Bros. 1941
FOUR JACKS AND A JILL — RKO Radio 1941
THAT UNCERTAIN FEELING — United Artists 1941 *scenes reshot
    with Alan Mowbray*
SLEEPYTIME GAL — Republic 1942
MAISIE GETS HER MAN — MGM 1942
ICELAND — 20th Century-Fox 1942
SHUT MY BIG MOUTH — Columbia 1942
PHANTOM OF THE OPERA — Universal 1943
HOLY MATRIMONY — 20th Century-Fox 1943
HENRY ALDRICH SWINGS IT — Paramount 1943
EVER SINCE VENUS — Columbia 1944
KNICKERBOCKER HOLIDAY — United Artists 1944
PASSPORT TO DESTINY (Passport to Adventure) — RKO Radio 1944
TAKE IT BIG — Paramount 1944
GEORGE WHITE'S SCANDALS — RKO Radio 1945
THE GREAT JOHN L. — United Artists 1945

In typical character make up, for *Victory* (1940).

CAPTAIN TUGBOAT ANNIE — Republic 1945
WIFE OF MONTE CRISTO — PRC 1946
CATMAN OF PARIS — Republic 1946
I'VE ALWAYS LOVED YOU — Republic 1946
HER SISTER'S SECRET — PRC 1946
GENTLEMAN JOE PALOOKA — Monogram 1946
THE SECRET LIFE OF WALTER MITTY — Goldwyn-RKO Radio 1947
CARNIVAL IN COSTA RICA — 20th Century-Fox 1947
FUN ON A WEEKEND — United Artists 1947
JULIA MISBEHAVES — MGM 1948
IF YOU KNEW SUSIE — RKO Radio 1948
MY GIRL TISA — Warner Bros. 1948
THE NOOSE HANGS HIGH — Eagle-Lion 1948
YOU GOTTA STAY HAPPY — Universal-International 1948
MEXICAN HAYRIDE — Universal-International 1948
TROUBLE MAKERS — Monogram 1948
THE LOVABLE CHEAT — Film Classics 1949

Clowning with Mel Brooks on the set of *Silent Movie* (1976).

THE GREAT LOVER — Paramount 1949
THE JACKPOT — 20th Century-Fox 1950
BELLE OF OLD MEXICO — Republic 1950
RIDING HIGH — Paramount 1950
APPOINTMENT WITH DANGER — Paramount 1951
LITTLE EGYPT — Universal-International 1951
MISSING WOMEN — Republic 1951
MY FAVORITE SPY — Paramount 1951
SKY HIGH — Lippert 1951
JOURNEY INTO LIGHT — 20th Century-Fox 1951
KENTUCKY JUBILEE — Lippert 1951
RHYTHM INN — Monogram 1951
O. HENRY'S FULL HOUSE (The Full House) — 20th Century-Fox 1952
HAS ANYBODY SEEN MY GAL? — Universal-International 1952
AARON SLICK FROM PUNKIN' CRICK — Paramount 1952
CALL ME MADAM — 20th Century-Fox 1953
THE STAR — 20th Century-Fox 1953
CRIME WAVE (The City Is Dark) — Warner Bros. 1954
LIVING IT UP — Paramount 1954
CASANOVA'S BIG NIGHT — Paramount 1954
RIDING SHOTGUN — Warner Bros. 1954
THE FRENCH LINE — RKO Radio 1954
PARIS PLAYBOYS — Allied Artists 1954
JAIL BUSTERS — Allied Artists 1955
UP IN SMOKE — Allied Artists 1957
JUKE BOX RHYTHM — Columbia 1959

DON'T GIVE UP THE SHIP — Paramount 1959
THE LADIES' MAN — Paramount 1961
POCKETFUL OF MIRACLES — United Artists 1961
ONE, TWO, THREE — United Artists 1961 *voice*
THE ERRAND BOY — Paramount 1962
WHO'S MINDING THE STORE? — Paramount 1963
WIVES AND LOVERS — Paramount 1963
FOUR FOR TEXAS — Warner Bros. 1963
THE MIRACLE OF SANTA'S WHITE REINDEER (The Miracle of the White
    Reindeer) — Gernos-Fantasy Films 1963
PROMISES! PROMISES! — Noonan-Taylor-NTD 1963
THE PATSY — Paramount 1964
HARLOW — Paramount 1965
THREE ON A COUCH — Columbia 1966
MADE IN PARIS — MGM 1966
WAY... WAY OUT — 20th Century-Fox 1966
FAME IS THE NAME OF THE GAME — Universal-NBC 1966 [TV movie]
PENELOPE — MGM 1966
CAPRICE — 20th Century-Fox 1967
BAREFOOT IN THE PARK — Paramount 1967
THE WICKED DREAMS OF PAULA SHULTZ — United Artists 1968
THE COMIC — Columbia 1969
HELLO, DOLLY! — 20th Century-Fox 1969
THE PHYNX — Warner Bros. 1970
WHICH WAY TO THE FRONT? — Warner Bros. 1970
THE COMPUTER WORE TENNIS SHOES — Disney-Buena Vista 1970
CALL HER MOM — Screen Gems-Columbia-ABC 1972 [TV movie]
ONLY WITH MARRIED MEN — Spelling-Goldberg-ABC 1974 [TV movie]
HERBIE RIDES AGAIN — Disney-Buena Vista 1974
THE STRONGEST MAN IN THE WORLD — Disney-Buena Vista 1975
THE SUNSHINE BOYS — MGM-United Artists 1975
WON TON TON, THE DOG WHO SAVED HOLLYWOOD —
    Paramount 1976
FREAKY FRIDAY — Disney-Buena Vista 1976
SILENT MOVIE — 20th Century-Fox 1976
THE WORLD'S GREATEST LOVER — 20th Century-Fox 1977
THE MAN YOU LOVE TO HATE — Film Profiles-BBC 1979
    [documentary]
HERBIE GOES BANANAS — Disney-Buena Vista 1980
HISTORY OF THE WORLD — PART I — 20th Century-Fox 1981
ALL THE MARBLES — MGM-United Artists 1981 *scenes deleted*
HEIDI'S SONG — Hanna Barbera-Paramount 1982 *voice*
LAST OF THE GREAT SURVIVORS — CBS 1984 [TV movie]
A FINE MESS — Columbia 1986 *scenes deleted*
TALKING PICTURES — BBC 1986 [documentary]

John Qualen

John Qualen stopped giving interviews a long time ago. I made several requests over the years, all of which were politely turned down. It was only when I gave up and simply invited him to lunch that he accepted. The conversation was informal, but he was more than willing to talk — and I was only too glad to listen. When he gave an impromptu performance in his living room — reprising a monolog from The Grapes of Wrath *— I was awed by the realism of it, and the tears he turned on and off at will.*

Little did John Qualen dream as a youth, that a gift for oratory and a flair for comedy would eventually lead to a career as one of Hollywood's most dependable character actors. Nor did he imagine that he would find a kind of immortality portraying pathetic little men with tortured souls, like the desperate gunman in *His Girl Friday* or the farmer forced off his land in *The Grapes of Wrath*. But he was determined, from the outset, to go his own way.

"Nobody ever studied acting in those days. Acting was a sin," says Qualen. "My father was a very strict man, a Norwegian Lutheran minister. He threatened to disown me if I became an actor, even tried to get my wife to talk me out of it — it didn' t make a particle of difference." Years later, he bought his parents a home in Los Angeles, and helped support his father. "He was tickled to death then," reports the actor.

Johan Mandt Kvalen (not John Oleson, as generally recorded) was born in Vancouver, British Columbia, on December 8, 1899. The future performer moved to the United States with his family when he was a year old. His grandfather, whose original surname was Olson, changed the name to Kvalen (meaning "flatland"); his father, in turn, changed the spelling to Qualen, "but everybody mispronounced it, so I changed the pronunciation."

The family moved a number of times while he was growing up, coinciding with his father's frequent change of congregation ("he had 'the wanders,'" notes Qualen). They stayed in Elgin, Illinois, long enough for Qualen to attend high school, where he studied oratory and flute and performed in comedy concerts.

"I sent away for a vaudeville sketch, and memorized it. I also did Swedish dialect stories," he recalls. "The dialect came easy; I grew up

87

With Will Rogers in *Doubting Thomas* (1934).

around it." Qualen also entered an oratory contest in Elgin, which won him a gold medal and a $1000 scholarship to Northwestern University.

When his father couldn't afford to finance his further education, the young man got a job as a tent boy on the Chautauqua circuit. One day the scheduled lecturer didn't show up, and Qualen offered to go on in his place. His talents prompted a show girl to send him to the eminent Elias Day of the Lyceum Arts Conservatory, whose pupils also included Robert Mitchum.

"He was the most extraordinary person I'd ever met," says Qualen. "He was a dynamo." After six months, Day sent him out on the road with two girl pianists. But when Qualen saw the conservatory going downhill, he went to New York to try his luck.

He made the rounds of New York agents, finding himself in the classic predicament: no experience, no job. "I finally said to one of them, 'How can I get experience on Broadway if no one will give me a job?' He said, 'It's tough, but that's your problem.'"

Qualen's opportunity finally came when Elmer Rice cast him as Olsen, the Swedish janitor in *Street Scene*. "Rice said, 'You're the man I'm looking for. I've been to every agent in town.' I said, 'I have too. They told me there were no jobs.'

"It was 1929, the heart of the depression," recalls the actor. "Good shows were folding every day. But *Street Scene* won the Pulitzer Prize and went on week after week and month after month." Five members of the original cast, including Qualen and Beulah Bondi,

With Paul Muni in *Black Fury* (1935).

were retained by Sam Goldwyn for the movie version.

The actor's screen debut caught the eye of John Ford, who cast him as a Swedish farmer in *Arrowsmith*. He then returned to New York, where he played a robbery suspect opposite Paul Muni in Elmer Rice's *Counsellor-at-Law* — another role he recreated in Hollywood.

"Muni was one of the greatest; I admired him tremendously. The play was so real to us, it was like we were living it — not acting," says Qualen. "John Barrymore played Paul's role in the film version. He couldn't remember his lines. I knew them from having done hundreds of stage performances; John started blowing his lines and then I started blowing mine."

Barrymore — whose performance in the 1933 film is regarded today as one of his best — was not the only performer with a faulty memory in Qualen's experience. "ZaSu Pitts was terrific," he says, "but she had a habit of whacking you in the chest when she forgot her lines."

The actor recalls with amusement the day Barrymore arrived with a hangover, having stayed up all night with John Gilbert. "He said to our director, William Wyler, 'God dammit, Willy, why don't you shoot this in a close-up? You know how you're going to cut this together.' He'd been up all night drinking. Wyler always called him John; he said, 'Mr. Barrymore, we're paying you $25,000 a week and you'll damn well do it the way we want it.'"

Qualen got so many film offers after *Counsellor-at-Law* that he moved to California. While he eventually played all types of characters on the screen, he found himself typecast as a Swede in the beginning. At one point, he and El Brendel — "he was on the skids when I came to Hollywood" — talked about working up a comedy act, The Two Swedes. "But he had a lot of ideas I didn't like," says Qualen.

He and child star Jane Withers were another team that didn't quite jell. "I made several pictures with her, but they [Fox] didn't have the right kind of material," he observes. "I needed something either very dramatic or very comic."

The actor's stock rose considerably in 1935 with his performances in *Black Fury*, as a coal miner who is beaten to death by police, and *Whipsaw*, as the father of a sick child. The latter led Darryl F. Zanuck to cast Qualen — by then a Fox contract player — as the father of the Dionne quintuplets in *Country Doctor*, which won him widespread recognition. But the role of Papa Dionne, a favorite he repeated in two sequels, typecast him for years as "the perennially frightened father or hen-pecked husband, caught up in circumstances beyond his control."

"Our doctor wondered how John could play an expectant father," says his wife of over 60 years, the former Pearle Larson. "He was on the road when our three daughters were born." But Qualen did his homework: "I went down to the maternity hospital and watched these poor guys, waiting for the children to be born."

The sequels to *Country Doctor* — *Reunion* and *Five of a Kind* — "were not very good," acknowledges Qualen, "but anything with the quints made a lot of money." At one point, actor Jean Hersholt warned him not to go up to Canada: "He told me, 'Dionne hates you for making him a laughing stock. He says you made a fool of him, fainting when the girls were born.' I don't know why he didn't like it," says the actor. "That's the way it was written, and that's the way I played it."

But, as he was guilty more than once, Qualen was a little too convincing in his portrayal of the quint's father. The film that followed *Country Doctor* — *The Road to Glory* (1936) — gave him a highly dramatic part as a crazed soldier. But the preview audience began to laugh when he appeared on screen, and the studio was forced to trim his part.

Qualen was kept so busy in the four decades that followed, he doesn't remember many of the films he did. "Fox put you into one after another; many of them were just two or three days work. I was ashamed of some of the pictures I did," says the actor, "but you didn't have any choice. Later, when I could afford to — when I didn't have to act in order to eat — I studied the script first."

As Muley Graves in *The Grapes of Wrath* (1940) — "John Ford had tears in his eyes when I did the scene."

As Axel Larson, with John Wayne in *The Long Voyage Home* (1940).

The year 1940 was a banner year for Qualen, providing him with three of his most memorable roles: Earl Williams, the escaped cop killer in Howard Hawks' *His Girl Friday*; Muley Graves, the displaced sharecropper in John Ford's film of John Steinbeck's *The Grapes of Wrath*; and Axel Larson, the homesick sailor in Ford's *The Long Voyage Home*. (He was asked to coach co-star John Wayne on his Swedish accent for the latter, but chose to decline the offer.)

The actor recalls *His Girl Friday* — which moves at break-neck pace — as "one of the best pictures I was in. You couldn't hear the lines at the preview, people were laughing so hard. Hawks completely ignored overlapping dialog. You generally let one person finish talking before the next one starts; he paid no attention to it all."

The unemployed bookkeeper-turned-desperado who hides in a newsman's roll-top desk was, alas, another part Qualen played too well. "Rosalind Russell was afraid of me," he reveals. "She told Hawks she didn't want me to have any bullets; she thought I was a little off. 'He's liable to shoot me,' she said." Hawks had to reassure her that Qualen was just acting.

With Douglas Fairbanks Jr. and Rita Hayworth in *Angels Over Broadway* (1940).

John Ford, who cast the actor in eight pictures — usually as a Norwegian or a Swede — "was wonderful with me," reports Qualen. "He had tears in his eyes when I did the scene in *The Grapes of Wrath* about my father working the land — the greatest scene I ever had in a picture."

But the director didn't always handle his actors properly, according to Qualen. "Barry Fitzgerald was a real artist, but Ford ruined him," declares the actor. "He bawled him out in front of everybody on *The Long Voyage Home*. He bawled the hell out of him: 'What the hell do you think we brought you all the way over from Ireland for?' Poor Barry couldn't perform. He was great in *Going My Way* — but Leo McCarey was very sensitive with him."

While he was never again to have the opportunities that 1940 presented him, Qualen was to remain almost frantically active throughout the remainder of his career. Though he was given few chances to stand in the spotlight, many a Hollywood director valued his services as an ensemble actor.

In *Casablanca*, he was an undercover spy working for Paul Henreid; in *Tortilla Flat*, he was a drunken paisano cavorting with Spencer Tracy. In *Two Rode Together*, he was a settler trying to rescue his daughter from the Indians; in *A Patch of Blue*, he was the kindly old merchant who befriended a blind Elizabeth Hartman.

He appeared on literally hundreds of television shows in the 1950s, '60s and '70s, including such programs as *Alfred Hitchcock Presents*, *The Danny Thomas Show*, *Ben Casey*, *I Spy*, *Green Acres*, *The Odd Couple* and *The Partridge Family*. Film and television work left him little time for the stage, although he played Mr. De Pinna in a 1950 production of *You Can't Take It With You*, at Hollywood's Las Palmas Theatre.

Regardless how small the role, Qualen was ever consistent in the quality of his work. Whether playing a rustic in a King Vidor Depression drama (*Our Daily Bread*) or a fireman in a William Wellman farce (*Nothing Sacred*), an embezzler (*Angels Over Broadway*) or a short order cook (*The Searchers*), his characterizations had a veracity few actors could match. He was as credible as an ailing senior citizen in a 1973 episode of TV's *The Streets of San Francisco*, as he was playing Aladdin of the magic lamp in *Arabian Nights* three decades earlier.

Despite the realism inherent in his portrayals, Qualen rarely — if ever — fell back on his own experience. "I didn't draw on myself for any of the parts I've played," he observes. "None of them are like me."

Although typecasting "kept me away from a lot of parts I could have played," John Qualen has few regrets. The one part he wanted but didn't get was that of an undertaker in *I Remember Mama*, a sentimental drama about a Norwegian family in the U.S. "I was very disappointed about that," he recalls. "Edgar Bergen got the role, because he had the name."

The actor, who retired to Torrance, California, in 1976, suffers from glaucoma and is hard of hearing. At 86, he is a man who takes due pride in his acting accomplishments — and his 10 grandchildren — but spends little time dwelling on the past. And while he is grateful to be remembered today, he wants no part of the limelight.

Toward the end of his career.

THE FILMS OF JOHN QUALEN

Qualen did not appear in THE GAY DECEPTION (1935) or THE COMANCHEROS (1961), as recorded elsewhere. Film clips of the actor were used in the documentary, AMERICA AT THE MOVIES (1976).

STREET SCENE — Goldwyn-United Artists 1931
ARROWSMITH — Goldwyn-United Artists 1931
COUNSELLOR-AT-LAW — Universal 1933
THE DEVIL'S BROTHER (Fra Diavolo) — Roach-MGM 1933
LET'S FALL IN LOVE — Columbia 1934
UPPER WORLD — Warner Bros. 1934
HI, NELLIE! — Warner Bros. 1934
SING AND LIKE IT — RKO Radio 1934
HE WAS HER MAN — Warner Bros. 1934
OUR DAILY BREAD — United Artists 1934
SERVANTS' ENTRANCE — Fox 1934
365 NIGHTS IN HOLLYWOOD — Fox 1934
STRAIGHT IS THE WAY (Four Walls) — MGM 1934
PRIVATE SCANDAL — Paramount 1934
NO GREATER GLORY (Men of Tomorrow) — Columbia 1934
ONE MORE SPRING — Fox 1935
THE GREAT HOTEL MURDER — Fox 1935
CHARLIE CHAN IN PARIS — Fox 1935
DOUBTING THOMAS — Fox 1935
ORCHIDS TO YOU — Fox 1935
THUNDER IN THE NIGHT — Fox 1935
THE FARMER TAKES A WIFE — Fox 1935
THE SILK HAT KID — Fox 1935
CHASING YESTERDAY — RKO Radio 1935
THE THREE MUSKETEERS — RKO Radio 1935
BLACK FURY — First National 1935
MAN OF IRON — First National 1935
CHEERS OF THE CROWD — Republic 1935
RING AROUND THE MOON — Chesterfield 1935
WHIPSAW — MGM 1935
THE COUNTRY DOCTOR — 20th Century-Fox 1936
THE ROAD TO GLORY — 20th Century-Fox 1936
GIRL'S DORMITORY — 20th Century-Fox 1936
REUNION — 20th Century-Fox 1936
MEET NERO WOLFE — Columbia 1936
WIFE VS. SECRETARY — MGM 1936
NOTHING SACRED — Selznick-United Artists 1937
SEVENTH HEAVEN — 20th Century-Fox 1937
FIFTY ROADS TO TOWN — 20th Century-Fox 1937
ANGEL'S HOLIDAY — 20th Century-Fox 1937
SHE HAD TO EAT — 20th Century-Fox 1937
FIT FOR A KING — RKO Radio 1937

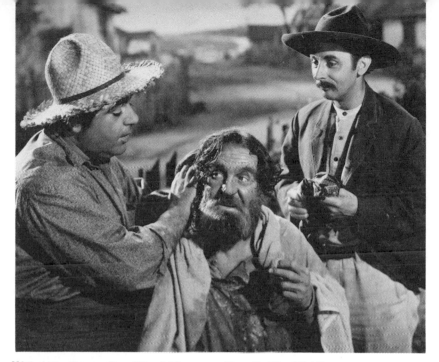

With Akim Tamiroff and Frank Morgan in *Tortilla Flat* (1942).

THE BAD MAN FROM BRIMSTONE — MGM 1938
THE CHASER — MGM 1938
JOY OF LIVING — RKO Radio 1938
FIVE OF A KIND — 20th Century-Fox 1938
THE MAD MISS MANTON — RKO Radio 1938
OUTSIDE THE LAW — Columbia 1938
THE TEXANS — Paramount 1938
LET US LIVE — Columbia 1939
STAND UP AND FIGHT — MGM 1939
MICKEY THE KID — Republic 1939
THUNDER AFLOAT — MGM 1939
FOUR WIVES — Warner Bros. 1939
HONEYMOON IN BALI (My Love for Yours) — Paramount 1939
HIS GIRL FRIDAY — Columbia 1940
BLONDIE ON A BUDGET — Columbia 1940
ANGELS OVER BROADWAY (Before I Die) — Columbia 1940
THE GRAPES OF WRATH — 20th Century-Fox 1940
ON THEIR OWN — 20th Century-Fox 1940
THE LONG VOYAGE HOME — United Artists 1940
YOUTH WILL BE SERVED — 20th Century-Fox 1940
SKI PATROL — Universal 1940
KNUTE ROCKNE — ALL-AMERICAN — Warner Bros. 1940
BABIES FOR SALE — Columbia 1940
BROTHER ORCHID — Warner Bros. 1940
OUT OF THE FOG — Warner Bros. 1941
MILLION DOLLAR BABY — Warner Bros. 1941

THE SHEPHERD OF THE HILLS — Paramount 1941
ALL THAT MONEY CAN BUY (The Devil and Daniel Webster, Here Is a
    Man) — RKO Radio 1941
NEW WINE (Melody Master) — United Artists 1941
MODEL WIFE — Universal 1941
LARCENY, INC. — Warner Bros. 1942
JUNGLE BOOK — United Artists 1942
TORTILLA FLAT — MGM 1942
ARABIAN NIGHTS — Universal 1942
CASABLANCA — Warner Bros. 1942
SWING SHIFT MAISIE — MGM 1943
THE IMPOSTOR (Bayonet Charge) — Universal 1944
AN AMERICAN ROMANCE — MGM 1944
DARK WATERS — United Artists 1944
ROUGHLY SPEAKING — Warner Bros. 1945
RIVER GANG (Fairy Tale Murder) — Universal 1945
CAPTAIN KIDD — United Artists 1945
ADVENTURE — MGM 1945
IT HAPPENED IN SPRINGFIELD — Warner Bros.-Vitaphone 1945 [short]
THE FUGITIVE — RKO Radio 1947
SONG OF SCHEHERAZADE — Universal 1947
HIGH CONQUEST — Monogram 1947
MY GIRL TISA — Warner Bros. 1948
ALIAS A GENTLEMAN — MGM 1948
ON OUR MERRY WAY (A Miracle Can Happen) — UA 1948
    scenes deleted
SIXTEEN FATHOMS DEEP — Monogram 1948
HOLLOW TRIUMPH (The Scar, The Man Who Murdered Himself) —
    Eagle-Lion 1948
THE BIG STEAL — RKO Radio 1949
CAPTAIN CHINA — Paramount 1949
CRISS CROSS — Universal 1949
BUCCANEER'S GIRL — Universal 1950
THE JACKPOT — 20th Century-Fox 1950
WOMAN ON THE RUN — Universal 1950
THE FLYING MISSILE — Columbia 1950
BELLE LE GRAND — Republic 1951
GOODBYE, MY FANCY — Warner Bros. 1951
HANS CHRISTIAN ANDERSEN — RKO Radio 1952
AMBUSH AT TOMAHAWK GAP — Columbia 1953
FRANCIS COVERS THE BIG TOWN — Universal-International 1953
I, THE JURY — United Artists 1953
THE STUDENT PRINCE — MGM 1954
THE HIGH AND THE MIGHTY — Warner Bros. 1954
PASSION — RKO Radio 1954
THE OTHER WOMAN — 20th Century-Fox 1954
UNCHAINED — Warner Bros. 1955
THE SEA CHASE — Warner Bros. 1955

With Elizabeth Hartman in *A Patch of Blue* (1965).

AT GUNPOINT — Allied Artists 1955
THE SEARCHERS — Warner Bros. 1956
JOHNNY CONCHO — United Artists 1956
THE BIG LAND — Warner Bros. 1957
THE GUN RUNNERS — United Artists 1958
TERROR IN THE HAUNTED HOUSE (My World Dies Screaming) —
    Howco International 1958
REVOLT IN THE BIG HOUSE — Allied Artists 1958
SO ALONE — British Film Institute 1958 [short]
ANATOMY OF A MURDER — Columbia 1959
NORTH TO ALASKA — 20th Century-Fox 1960
HELL BENT FOR LEATHER — Universal 1960
ELMER GANTRY — UA 1960
TWO RODE TOGETHER — Columbia 1961
THE MAN WHO SHOT LIBERTY VALANCE — Paramount 1962
THE PRIZE — MGM 1963
THE SEVEN FACES OF DR. LAO — MGM 1964
CHEYENNE AUTUMN — Warner Bros. 1964
THOSE CALLOWAYS — Disney-Buena Vista 1964
A PATCH OF BLUE — MGM 1965
THE SONS OF KATIE ELDER — Paramount 1965
I'LL TAKE SWEDEN — United Artists 1965
THE ADVENTURES OF BULLWHIP GRIFFIN — Disney-Buena Vista 1966
A BIG HAND FOR THE LITTLE LADY — Warner Bros. 1966
P.J. — Universal 1968
FIRECREEK — Warner Bros.-Seven Arts 1968
HAIL, HERO! — National General 1969
GETTING AWAY FROM IT ALL — Palomar-ABC 1972 [TV movie]
FRASIER, THE SENSUOUS LION — LCS 1973

Charles Lane

The abiding image of Charles Lane is so cold and nasty that one might expect a visit with him to be an unpleasant experience. And one would be wrong. Once I pulled him away from the golf course I found him a most congenial host, a man possessed of culture and even charm. He is candid and down-to-earth, and has a talent for self-deprecating remarks that would disarm most anyone.

One quick glimpse at his sour face tells the viewer that uninvited guest has come to foreclose the mortgage, repossess the car, audit the tax return or issue a subpoena. At 81, Charles Lane remains the epitome of the tight-lipped, thick-skinned, stingy old SOB.

"I think that started with *I Love Lucy*," says the actor, who has carved a niche for himself portraying such loathsome characters in films and television. "I always played some sort of a jerk on Lucille Ball's shows. They were all good parts — but they were all jerks."

Although he is a versatile, stage-trained performer, Lane has come to accept the "stinker" image over the years. "Our gorgeous type-casting is one of the most destructive things for an actor we've ever had," he says, "and it'll continue always. It's frustrating, but you have to resign yourself to that; you can't fight it and be miserable all the time. Besides, if you have a type established, and you're any good, it can mean considerable work for you."

Lane, who began his film career in 1931, feels his mental attitude has far more to do with his durability in Hollywood than any particular stereotype. "I have a very healthy attitude about casting," he contends. "I've always felt that it's none of my business. My business is to produce when I get there.

"I can go to an interview, not get it, and actually forget it driving back in the car. I've got friends who say, 'Damn it, I'd be better than he is in the part.' I say, 'Who gives a shit? It's not your province, It's the casting director's.'"

A native of San Francisco, Charles Gerstle Levison was born January 26, 1905 (he made the name change circa 1935, on the advice of his agent). There has been much confusion over his date of birth and his entry into films because of a silent film actor, "an old goat by the name of Charles Lane who died just when I came on the scene, or shortly afterward."

101

The son of a businessman, young Lane received a solid education in the arts. "My father had an artistic side to him; he was one of the founders of the San Francisco Symphony, and also the opera company. That's one clue as to why I went into the theater," says Lane. "I have three brothers, all businessmen. I was sort of the weird one."

He credits Irving Pichel — a prominent actor himself — for getting him started. While Lane was "fiddling around in the insurance business, and doing it much more harm than good," the two of them did a semi-professional show in San Francisco. Pichel thought he showed promise, and persuaded the young actor to travel to Los Angeles; together they joined the company at the Pasadena Playhouse in 1928.

"It was an outstanding theater, and many of the important people in our business started there," says Lane, who met his wife Ruth in the company. Two years after his arrival in Los Angeles, he found himself cast in a film called *Smart Money* with Edward G. Robinson.

"I haven't the vaguest idea how I got into pictures," says Lane. "I'm sure it happened this way — some director saw me at the Playhouse, and wanted to use me in his picture. Producers and directors from Hollywood came regularly to the Playhouse; it was a source of a great deal of talent."

Lane remained with the company while getting a foothold in the film business, as did many of his colleagues. "We were a healthy bunch of kids," he says. "We'd play at night and then clean up afterwards; then we'd go someplace and tell lies for an hour or two, and have to be in Hollywood at 7 o'clock in the morning. I did that for years; it was a marvelous background for a performer," asserts Lane, who eventually became head of production at the nationally renowned theater under founder Gilmor Brown.

The young actor made his first 18 film appearances at Warner Bros. — which got more than their money's worth, according to Lane. "When I started in pictures," he recalls, "my salary was $35 a day. I'd go over on Stage 26 at 11 o'clock and play an elevator operator with four lines, and at 3 o'clock another one. Then I'd go over to stage 13 and do a taxi driver with four lines. I'd often do three pictures in one day, all for the same $35. That was before we had the Screen Actors Guild."

Apart from a trio of Busby Berkeley musicals, Lane did little of substance at Warners. In 1934, he won two noteworthy roles at Columbia. On Howard Hawks' *Twentieth Century*, he nearly lost the role of hotshot producer Max Jacobs to George E. Stone.

"Apparently, Stone had a conflict; he was on something else and didn't finish, so I got it," says Lane. "Well, if you can picture a young

With John Barrymore and Carole Lombard in *Twentieth Century* (1934).

actor realizing that now, on Monday, he's going to play with John Barrymore... I walked the entire weekend in absolute terror all over the house.

"Not only to a young actor was the name enough to scare the shit out of you, but he also had a reputation as being a little bit of an ogre. The thing I was always stuck with, I always played the scene with the big star. I could never play it with the second lead, or the character man, so I went through my whole life in terror. And the opening shot of this picture — what they called 'the champagne shot' — was between the little poop and the giant.

"Monday, Hawks introduces the cast and I walk away stiff-legged, I'm so scared," says Lane. "And I hear behind me, 'Pssst!' I thought, 'Oh, shit, here it comes.' I started over to Barrymore. He says, 'Off the set, you little four-eyed jerk.' He takes me way over to the side of the set, behind some flat, where nobody could see us, and he says, 'Young man...'

"I said, 'Yes, sir?' He said, 'In this scene we're going to make, be loud. If you're loud, they won't notice me; I stink in it.' I looked him in the eye; I thought maybe it was a rib, but it wasn't. Barrymore had a total lack of security. He used to say, 'Some night in the theater, the whole audience is going to get wise to this phony at the same time

Talking taxes with Lionel Barrymore in *You Can't Take it With You* (1938).

and climb over the footlights and garrote him.'"

Three months later Lane was back at Columbia, playing a crooked gambler in *Broadway Bill* — the first of nine pictures in a 17-year association with Frank Capra. And while he has worked with virtually every director who ever passed through Hollywood in the past 55 years, Capra — not surprisingly — remains the actor's favorite.

"I'm prejudiced, I'll say that from the start. But I think Frank is the most talented man we ever had," contends Lane. "He knew the camera department as well or better than the head cameraman; he knew the sound department better than the head mixer. He had an intuitive feeling with scripts. On top of that, he had this marvelous ability to relate.

"Leo McCarey had a wonderful touch; I used to love working with him. Howard Hawks was another favorite of mine. There were many others, like George Seaton. But Frank had more talent in more areas as a director than anybody I knew," says Lane. "His casting used to amaze me.

"The phone would ring. The voice would say, 'Charlie? This is Frank Capra. I know it's a helluva thing to get you off the golf course, but could you come in and see me?' You'd say, 'Well, I might be able to squeeze it in.' You'd roar over to Columbia. The secretary would say, 'Oh, yes, Mr. Capra's expecting you.' You'd walk in and there the

With Angela Lansbury and Van Johnson in *State of the Union* (1948).

little wop would be, sitting all by himself, and he'd say, 'Look, maybe this would be fun, maybe it wouldn't, I don't know...' And that's the way he'd cast you."

When an actor arrived on the set of a Capra film, says Lane, he was secure in the knowledge that "Frank thought you were the best person for the part. He never contacted casting directors, or agents, or anybody. He knew everybody in town. Casting is ludicrous today; you go through these incredible interviews."

While Capra was the sole authority on his set, he never abused his power, according to Lane. Nor was the director anything but patient with actors, as illustrated by an incident with Gary Cooper during *Mr. Deeds Goes to Town.*

"I was a punk kid," says Lane, "and also a little deprecating toward pictures because I was a theater man. Coop and I rehearsed the scene, I read the first line, and the answer came back... you couldn't hear him. I thought, 'What the hell is this?' The next line, I projected a little more, and the answer was still inaudible. By the time we played the scene, I was really giving it, trying to get this guy to come on already.

"The next day Frank said, 'Do me a favor — come in and look at the dailies.' I was suspicious, so I took a seat way in the back of the projection room. Here came the scene, with this idiotic monkey on a stick [Lane] and this marvelous stuff [Cooper] underneath.

"Coop was gorgeous, and this jackass was terribly out of balance. Capra could, at that moment, have destroyed me, because I was humiliated that I'd made such an ass of myself. But instead, as we walked back to the set, he said, 'Eh! We'll do it again tomorrow.'"

Capra never typed the actor — as so many others did — casting Lane in such memorable roles as the flustered Internal Revenue agent in *You Can't Take It With You*, and the obnoxious reporter in *Mr. Smith Goes to Washington* ("Any special axes to grind, Senator?"). As a result, the director always inspired him to do his best.

"You break your ass for someone like Capra or Hawks," says Lane. "You try to be as good as you can when you have a relationship with a director like that. The others, you have this 'get it over with and get out of here' attitude."

In the six-year period from 1936 through 1941, Lane acted in an astonishing total of 125 pictures (31 alone in '41 — his busiest year ever). "To make as many pictures as I did," he points out, "we had to work in these B-units, like the Sol Wurtzel unit at Fox. We used to run around and do these stinking musicals — we did horrible things at Paramount.

"That was when every town in the country had a picture house, and they changed the bill in the middle of the week; they had to have four pictures a week. They'd make these damn things in 15 or 18 days, and the only people who saw 'em were these people out in the sticks that went to a double feature. That's where an actor like myself piled up so many credits."

In between the "18-day wonders," Lane acted in first-rate films with Hollywood's finest. "Every one of the big people I worked with — and I guess I worked with practically all of them — were 100% pros," claims the actor. "I've never worked with an important person in our business that I didn't think was an absolute delight to work with.

"I did a lot of pictures with Clark Gable. I was very fond of Clark; he was a very special person," says Lane. "But he was a man of great insecurity in his work. Once we were shooting over at the old Wilshire Ebell theater. Clark was at the peak of his career.

"We went to lunch — I wasn't very hungry, so I came back about a half hour early. There were three grips eating their sandwiches out of paper bags, and Gable — rehearsing all by himself. I said, 'What in God's name are you doing?' He said, 'Oh, Charlie, I stink so in this thing, I've got to do something about it.' That was his attitude; he was a very hard worker."

Lane too was a hard worker, busying himself with television when

As Detective Burns in *The Mysterious Intruder* (1946).

With Jim Backus in *Billie* (1965).

film production began to wane in the early 1950s. The actor's five-year stint as railroad magnate Homer Bedloe on *Petticoat Junction*, beginning in 1963, made him a familiar face to millions of TV viewers. His recurring role as a crusty old judge on the 1977-78 season of *Soap* introduced him to a new generation.

Despite the fact that television has been his bread and butter for over three decades, Lane has never been enamored of the medium. "I've always quarreled with the three-camera method of production on TV. Jess Oppenheimer, who produced *I Love Lucy*, created the concept; I've never forgiven him for it. We used to make those things in three days: The first day you read the script and did a little blocking. The second day was usually taken up entirely with arguments. And the third day, you did it."

"I think TV embodies the worst of theater and the worst of motion pictures all in one medium," he declares. "Now they rehearse five days and do two shows, for two different audiences, so you have two cracks at it — but I still don't like it. There's only one reason for it, and don't let anybody tell you there's any other: It's cheap! And it stinks."

While he once made what he now considers a "fat-headed remark" about having no interest in films once finished with them, Lane can't stand to watch himself on screen. "I studiously avoid seeing myself, especially on TV, because it's always so half-assed," he says. "I like the classic films better, but I've never liked myself. I look at it as me doing a job."

Since the advent of cable television, Lane turns up constantly on the tube. The intrepid viewer will spot him "doing a job" anywhere and everywhere: as an anxious playwright in *42nd Street*, a photographer in *Professor Beware*, a furniture salesman in *Blondie*; as Dr. Prouty in Columbia's *Ellery Queen* series, a rent collector in *It's a Wonderful Life*, the prosecuting attorney in *Call Northside 777*. In *The Big Store* he's the man who repossesses Groucho Marx' car; in *Good Neighbor Sam*, he hires a detective to spy on Jack Lemmon.

The venerable actor, who made his Broadway debut in Norman Krasna's *Love in E Flat* (1967) — and subsequently played the title role in a UCLA production of *The Man Who Came to Dinner* — has derived his greatest satisfaction from the theater, in terms of the parts he's played.

Though he enjoys reminiscing, he is quick to point out, "I am not one of these old goats who dwells on the past and says, 'The great old days...' — because the great old days, a lot of them stunk. But those big stars — and I don't use that word loosely; in the heyday of pictures, we had maybe a dozen of them — they were bigger than life, those people. When Gable walked into the MGM commissary, silence descended over the room. It takes some kind of presence to project that. Clark was totally unaware of it, but he had that quality; quite a few of them did. I don't see that anymore."

A few years ago, Lane returned to MGM to do "some cops-and-robbers thing" with a group of young unknowns. "They'd gotten delusions of grandeur. They were telling the cameraman where to put the camera, the director how to direct it. You looked at them with some sadness — this was their first job and obviously would be their last. This is a pretty humble business," asserts Lane. "Acting is a cruel profession: here today, gone tomorrow. Unless you can make peace with the cruelty of Hollywood, you don't belong here."

Lane, who puts in a 40-hour week on the golf course when not acting, has made his peace with "the cruelest town that ever existed." While his memory has receded along with his hairline, he has no trouble learning his lines. "It's weird," he says. "As you get older, you can't remember a bloody thing. But I've always been a very fast study and that's unimpaired."

Still busy in television, he was seen as Admiral Stanley in *The Winds of War*, and is slated to reprise his role in the upcoming sequel, *War and Remembrance*. In films, he starred as a kindly grandfather in *The Little Dragons* and more recently had a cameo in *Murphy's Romance*.

"If you get a feature film now, it's out of the blue. There aren't many parts written for old goats," concedes the octogenarian, "but you try and stay as active as you can."

photo by the author

"I must have played nice guys, but not an awful lot."

THE FILMS OF CHARLES LANE

Most reference books confuse the Charles Lane featured in this book with a silent film actor by the same name. The former did not appear in any film released prior to 1931; he was billed as Charles Levison until the mid-'30s. Lane did not appear in NEVER GIVE A SUCKER AN EVEN BREAK (1941), MEET JOHN DOE (1941), DUDES ARE PRETTY PEOPLE (1942), MR. LUCKY (1943) or MODELS, INC. (1952), as recorded elsewhere; Charles *Lang* was in the former, Charles *Cane* in the latter two. Based on a list compiled by Lane, and other sources.

SMART MONEY — Warner Bros. 1931
ROAD TO SINGAPORE — Warner Bros. 1931
BLONDE CRAZY (Larceny Lane) — Warner Bros. 1931
MANHATTAN PARADE — Warner Bros. 1932
UNION DEPOT — First National 1932
THE MOUTHPIECE — Warner Bros. 1932
BLESSED EVENT — First National 1932
CENTRAL AIRPORT (Hello, Central) — First National 1933
GRAND SLAM — Warner Bros. 1933
42ND STREET — Warner Bros. 1933
EMPLOYEE'S ENTRANCE — First National 1933
THE KING'S VACATION — Warner Bros. 1933
BLONDIE JOHNSON — First National 1933
THE SILK EXPRESS — Warner Bros. 1933
PRIVATE DETECTIVE 62 (Man Killer) — Warner Bros. 1933
GOLD DIGGERS OF 1933 — Warner Bros. 1933
FOOTLIGHT PARADE — Warner Bros. 1933
MY WOMAN — Columbia 1933
THE BOWERY — United Artists 1933
MR. SKITCH — Fox 1933
ADVICE TO THE LOVELORN — United Artists 1933
SHE HAD TO SAY YES — First National 1933 *scenes deleted*
SHOW-OFF — MGM 1934
TWENTY MILLION SWEETHEARTS (Hot Air, Rhythm in the Air) —
     First National 1934
LOOKING FOR TROUBLE — United Artists 1934
TWENTIETH CENTURY — Columbia 1934
BROADWAY BILL — Columbia 1934
I'LL FIX IT — Columbia 1934
THE BAND PLAYS ON — MGM 1934
A WICKED WOMAN — MGM 1934
LET'S TALK IT OVER — Universal 1934
ONE MORE SPRING — Fox 1935
PRINCESS O'HARA — Universal 1935
GINGER — Fox 1935

111

TWO FOR TONIGHT — Paramount 1935
HERE COMES THE BAND — MGM 1935
I LIVE MY LIFE — MGM 1935
THE MILKY WAY — Paramount 1936
IT HAD TO HAPPEN — 20th Century-Fox 1936
MR. DEEDS GOES TO TOWN — Columbia 1936
NEIGHBORHOOD HOUSE — Roach-MGM 1936
THE CRIME OF DR. FORBES — 20th Century-Fox 1936
TICKET TO PARADISE — Republic 1936
36 HOURS TO KILL (36 Hours to Live) — 20th Century-Fox 1936
THREE MEN ON A HORSE — First National 1936
EASY TO TAKE — Paramount 1936
COME CLOSER, FOLKS — Columbia 1936
BORN TO DANCE — MGM 1936
LADY LUCK — Chesterfield 1936
TWO-FISTED GENTLEMAN — Columbia 1936
THE BRIDE WALKS OUT — RKO Radio 1936
BAD GUY — MGM 1937
THE JONES FAMILY IN HOT WATER — 20th Century-Fox 1937
THE JONES FAMILY IN BIG BUSINESS — 20th Century-Fox 1937
SEA DEVILS (Coast Patrol) — RKO Radio 1937
VENUS MAKES TROUBLE — Columbia 1937
BORN RECKLESS (Armored Taxi) — 20th Century-Fox 1937
ONE MILE FROM HEAVEN — 20th Century-Fox 1937
CRIMINAL LAWYER — RKO Radio 1937
WE'RE ON THE JURY — RKO Radio 1937
INTERNES CAN'T TAKE MONEY — Paramount 1937
BROADWAY MELODY OF 1938 — MGM 1937
FIT FOR A KING — RKO Radio 1937
NOTHING SACRED — Selznick-United Artists 1937
ALI BABA GOES TO TOWN — 20th Century-Fox 1937
DANGER! LOVE AT WORK — 20th Century-Fox 1937
PARTNERS IN CRIME — Paramount 1937
TRAPPED BY G-MEN (River of Missing Men) — Columbia 1937
INSIDE STORY — 20th Century-Fox 1938
IN OLD CHICAGO — 20th Century-Fox 1938
HAVING WONDERFUL TIME — RKO Radio 1938
CITY GIRL — 20th Century-Fox 1938
JOY OF LIVING — RKO Radio 1938
PROFESSOR BEWARE — Paramount 1938
COCOANUT GROVE — Paramount 1938
THE RAGE OF PARIS — Universal 1938
YOU CAN'T TAKE IT WITH YOU — Columbia 1938
ALWAYS IN TROUBLE — 20th Century-Fox 1938
THREE LOVES HAS NANCY — MGM 1938
BLONDIE — Columbia 1938
KENTUCKY — 20th Century-Fox 1938

With George Cleveland (left), Fortunio Bonanova and George Chandler in *Obliging Young Lady* (1941).

THANKS FOR EVERYTHING — 20th Century-Fox 1938
THE UNEXPECTED FATHER — Universal 1939
THE HONEYMOON'S OVER — 20th Century-Fox 1939
THINK IT OVER — MGM 1939 [short]
MADE FOR EACH OTHER — Selznick-United Artists 1939
BOY SLAVES — RKO Radio 1939
LET US LIVE — Columbia 1939
THE FLYING IRISHMAN — RKO Radio 1939
LUCKY NIGHT — MGM 1939
NEWS IS MADE AT NIGHT — 20th Century-Fox 1939
ROSE OF WASHINGTON SQUARE — 20th Century-Fox 1939
THE CAT AND THE CANARY — Paramount 1939
MR. SMITH GOES TO WASHINGTON — Columbia 1939
SECOND FIDDLE — 20th Century-Fox 1939
GOLDEN BOY — Columbia 1939
THUNDER AFLOAT — MGM 1939
MIRACLES FOR SALE — MGM 1939
FIFTH AVENUE GIRL — RKO Radio 1939
HONEYMOON IN BALI (My Love for Yours) — Paramount 1939
ANOTHER THIN MAN — MGM 1939
CHARLIE McCARTHY, DETECTIVE — Universal 1939

THE ICE FOLLIES OF 1939 — MGM 1939
THE JONES FAMILY IN HOLLYWOOD — 20th Century-Fox 1939
BEWARE, SPOOKS! — Columbia 1939
TELEVISION SPY (World on Parade) — Paramount 1939
THEY ALL COME OUT — MGM 1939
THE FLAG SPEAKS — MGM 1940 [short]
ALIAS THE DEACON — Universal 1940
A LITTLE BIT OF HEAVEN — Universal 1940
SANDY IS A LADY — Universal 1940
BUCK BENNY RIDES AGAIN — Paramount 1940
JOHNNY APOLLO — 20th Century-Fox 1940
THE PRIMROSE PATH — RKO Radio 1940
QUEEN OF THE MOB — Paramount 1940
DOCTOR TAKES A WIFE — Columbia 1940
IT'S A DATE — Universal 1940
ON THEIR OWN — 20th Century-Fox 1940
YOU CAN'T FOOL YOUR WIFE — RKO Radio 1940
EDISON, THE MAN — MGM 1940
THE CROOKED ROAD — Republic 1940
WE WHO ARE YOUNG — MGM 1940
DANCING ON A DIME — Paramount 1940
THE TEXAS RANGERS RIDE AGAIN — Paramount 1940
RHYTHM ON THE RIVER — Paramount 1940
CITY FOR CONQUEST — Warner Bros. 1940
THE GREAT PROFILE — 20th Century-Fox 1940
THE LEATHER PUSHERS — Universal 1940
BLONDIE PLAYS CUPID — Columbia 1940
ELLERY QUEEN, MASTER DETECTIVE — Columbia 1940
PAROLE FIXER — Paramount 1940
I CAN'T GIVE YOU ANYTHING BUT LOVE, BABY — Universal 1940
YOUNG AS YOU FEEL — 20th Century-Fox 1940
THE INVISIBLE WOMAN — Universal 1940
YOU'RE THE ONE — Paramount 1941
FOOTLIGHT FEVER — RKO Radio 1941
NEW YORK TOWN — Paramount 1941 *scenes deleted*
BACK STREET — Universal 1941
ELLERY QUEEN'S PENTHOUSE MYSTERY — Columbia 1941
SIS HOPKINS — Republic 1941
REPENT AT LEISURE — RKO Radio 1941
BUY ME THAT TOWN — Paramount 1941
ELLERY QUEEN AND THE PERFECT CRIME — Columbia 1941
THE BIG STORE — MGM 1941
OBLIGING YOUNG LADY — RKO Radio 1941
BARNACLE BILL — MGM 1941
BALL OF FIRE — Goldwyn-RKO Radio 1941
APPOINTMENT FOR LOVE — Universal 1941
BIRTH OF THE BLUES — Paramount 1941

LOOK WHO'S LAUGHING — RKO Radio 1941
I WAKE UP SCREAMING (Hot Spot) — 20th Century-Fox 1941
CONFIRM OR DENY — 20th Century-Fox 1941
SING ANOTHER CHORUS — Universal 1941
SHE KNEW ALL THE ANSWERS — Columbia 1941
BLONDIE IN SOCIETY — Columbia 1941
THREE GIRLS ABOUT TOWN — Columbia 1941
SEALED LIPS (Beyond the Law) — Columbia 1941
FLYING TIGERS — Republic 1942
RIDE 'EM COWBOY — Universal 1942
ENEMY AGENTS MEET ELLERY QUEEN — Columbia 1942
A GENTLEMAN AT HEART — 20th Century-Fox 1942
ABOUT FACE — Roach-United Artists 1942
FRIENDLY ENEMIES — United Artists 1942
BROADWAY — Universal 1942
LADY IN A JAM — Universal 1942
PARDON MY SARONG — Universal 1942
THRU DIFFERENT EYES — 20th Century-Fox 1942
HOME IN WYOMIN' — Republic 1942
THE LADY IS WILLING — Columbia 1942
TARZAN'S NEW YORK ADVENTURE — MGM 1942
THE GREAT MAN'S LADY — Paramount 1942
THEY ALL KISSED THE BRIDE — Columbia 1942
BORN TO SING — MGM 1942
THE MAD MARTINDALES — 20th Century-Fox 1942
ARE HUSBANDS NECESSARY? — Paramount 1942
THE ADVENTURES OF MARTIN EDEN — Columbia 1942
WHAT'S COOKIN' (Wake Up and Dream) — Universal 1942
YOKEL BOY (Movie Yokel) — Republic 1942
ARSENIC AND OLD LACE — Warner Bros. 1944
A CLOSE CALL FOR BOSTON BLACKIE — Columbia 1946
THE INVISIBLE INFORMER — Republic 1946
THE SHOW-OFF — MGM 1946
IT'S A WONDERFUL LIFE — Liberty Films-RKO Radio 1946
JUST BEFORE DAWN — Columbia 1946
THE MYSTERIOUS INTRUDER (Murder Is Unpredictable) —
    Columbia 1946
I COVER BIG TOWN (I Cover the Underworld) — Paramount 1947
IT HAPPENED ON 5TH AVENUE — Monogram-Allied Artists 1947
SWELL GUY — Universal 1947
LOUISIANA — Monogram 1947
ROSES ARE RED — 20th Century-Fox 1947
THE FARMER'S DAUGHTER — RKO Radio 1947
LIVING IN A BIG WAY — MGM 1947
INTRIGUE — United Artists 1947
BURY ME DEAD — Eagle Lion 1947
RACE STREET — RKO Radio 1948

With Paul Guilfoyle in *Roses Are Red* (1947).

CALL NORTHSIDE 777 (Calling Northside 777) — 20th Century-Fox 1948
SMART WOMAN — Monogram-Allied Artists 1948
STATE OF THE UNION — Liberty Films-MGM 1948
APARTMENT FOR PEGGY — 20th Century-Fox 1948
MOONRISE — Republic 1948
GENTLEMAN FROM NOWHERE — Columbia 1948
OUT OF THE STORM — Republic 1948
STREETS OF SAN FRANCISCO — Republic 1949
MOTHER IS A FRESHMAN — 20th Century-Fox 1949
YOU'RE MY EVERYTHING — 20th Century-Fox 1949
MISS GRANT TAKES RICHMOND — Columbia 1949
MIGHTY JOE YOUNG — RKO Radio 1949
THE HOUSE ACROSS THE STREET — Warner Bros. 1949
ROOKIE FIREMAN — Columbia 1950
RIDING HIGH — Paramount 1950
BORDERLINE — Universal-International 1950
THE YELLOW CAB MAN — MGM 1950
LOVE THAT BRUTE — 20th Century-Fox 1950
BACKFIRE — Warner Bros. 1950
FOR HEAVEN'S SAKE — 20th Century-Fox 1950
WATCH THE BIRDIE — MGM 1950
CRIMINAL LAWYER — Columbia 1951
HERE COMES THE GROOM — Paramount 1951
I CAN GET IT FOR YOU WHOLESALE — 20th Century-Fox 1951
THE DuPONT STORY — Modern Talking Pictures 1952 [documentary]

THREE FOR BEDROOM C — Warner Bros. 1952
THE SNIPER — Columbia 1952
THE AFFAIRS OF DOBIE GILLIS — MGM 1953
REMAINS TO BE SEEN — MGM 1953
THE JUGGLER — Columbia 1953
THE BIRDS AND THE BEES — Paramount 1956
TOP SECRET AFFAIR — Warner Bros. 1957
GOD IS MY PARTNER — 20th Century-Fox 1957
TEACHER'S PET — Paramount 1958
THE MATING GAME — MGM 1959
BUT NOT FOR ME — Paramount 1959
THE 30-FOOT BRIDE OF CANDY ROCK — Columbia 1959
ALCATRAZ EXPRESS — Desilu-Paramount 1962 [comprised of
    Untouchables TV episodes]
THE MUSIC MAN — Warner Bros. 1962
PAPA'S DELICATE CONDITION — Paramount 1963
IT'S A MAD, MAD, MAD, MAD WORLD — United Artists 1963
THE WHEELER DEALERS — MGM 1963
GOOD NEIGHBOR SAM — Columbia 1964
THE CARPETBAGGERS — Paramount 1964
THE NEW INTERNS — Columbia 1964
LOOKING FOR LOVE — MGM 1964
JOHN GOLDFARB, PLEASE COME HOME — 20th Century-Fox 1965
BILLIE — United Artists 1965
THE UGLY DACHSHUND — Disney-Buena Vista 1966
THE GHOST AND MR. CHICKEN — Universal 1966
THE GNOME-MOBILE — Disney-Buena Vista 1967
EIGHT ON A LAM — United Artists 1967
WHAT'S SO BAD ABOUT FEELING GOOD? — Universal 1968
DID YOU HEAR THE ONE ABOUT THE TRAVELING SALESLADY?
    — Universal 1968
THE ARISTOCATS — Disney-Buena Vista 1970 *voice*
GET TO KNOW YOUR RABBIT — Warner Bros. 1972
THE GREAT MAN'S WHISKERS — NBC 1973 [TV movie]
HITCHED — NBC 1973 [TV movie]
SYBIL — NBC 1976 [TV movie]
MOVIE MOVIE — Warner Bros. 1978
EVERY WHICH WAY BUT LOOSE — Warner Bros. 1978
THE LITTLE DRAGONS — Aurora 1980
RETURN OF THE BEVERLY HILLBILLIES — CBS 1981 [TV movie]
STRANGE BEHAVIOR — World Northal 1981
THE WINDS OF WAR — ABC 1983 [TV movie]
SUNSET LIMOUSINE — CBS 1983 [TV movie]
STRANGE INVADERS — Orion-Warner Bros. 1983
MURPHY'S ROMANCE — Columbia 1986

Anita Garvin

Anita Garvin had not given an interview in 40 years when she invited me to her home. She was a little apprehensive about "going public," but there was none of the haughty demeanor one associates with the characters she played; she is as warm in person as she was icy on screen. She remains modest and unassuming, overwhelmed by the adulation that has greeted her in recent years; her fans are legion, their affection genuine.

Few actresses of the 1920s and '30s, blessed with her face and figure, had the desire to indulge in knockabout comedy. Fewer still were willing to sit on a custard pie, jump into a free-for-all with a seltzer bottle or play a scene with a rambunctious chimpanzee. And virtually no one has ever taken a pratfall as gracefully as Anita Garvin.

To Stan Laurel, she was a pioneer. To Florenz Ziegfeld, one of the most beautiful girls in the world. To the cognoscenti — and to Laurel and Hardy fans in particular — Garvin ranks as the uncrowned queen of slapstick. To this day, she is deluged with fan mail; when she suffered a heart attack in 1983, get well cards poured in from around the world.

Film historian Leonard Maltin has called her "one of the screen's finest, and unjustly forgotten comediennes... a beautiful woman with a mobile and expressive face, and timing that could put many experienced comedians to shame." In his later years, Stan Laurel told her, "When I get well, I'm going to do my best to get you a star on Hollywood Boulevard."

Born February 11, 1907 in New York City, Anita Garvin was stagestruck as far back as she can recall. "I remember crawling up the fire escape of Loew's American Theater at 42nd and Broadway, looking in the actresses' dressing room and watching them make up. There was a benefit at the Met when I was 7 or 8; the three Barrymores were there. There was a big crowd at the stage door and I got pushed around. They got in a cab and I got thrown in that cab, on my head. They were so nice — that was my big thrill."

Garvin was first encouraged by a pair of sisters who lived in her apartment building and sang and danced in vaudeville shows. "They were very nice to me. They'd teach me different steps, and I'd go and practice with them. One day they went downtown to an agent; they went in and five minutes later they had booking. I thought, 'Well, that's easy.'

"The next day I put my hair up and I went and saw the same man. He says, 'How old are you?' I said, '16.' He says, '*How old?*' I said, 'Well, *almost* 16.' Anita, who was a precocious 12 — and had already attained her full height of 5 feet, 6 inches — found work that same afternoon, as a Mack Sennett Bathing Beauty in a live stage show.

"I saw the man at 10 o'clock that morning and at 1 o'clock I was on stage," she marvels. "I was the only girl in the show who wasn't a real Sennett girl — one girl got homesick and left, and they had to have somebody fill in. While I was with the company Jesse Lasky offered to bring my mother and myself to Hollywood to go into pictures. I was to get $75 a week."

Her mother turned down the offer; Anita was too young to be traipsing the stage in a fur-lined bathing suit and high heels, much less go to Hollywood. Garvin's first professional job also did not endear her to the Gerry Society, which enforced the child labor laws at that time.

But Anita, who posed for artist James Montgomery Flagg about the same time, was undaunted. By the tender age of 13 she was appearing in Ziegfeld's *Midnight Frolic* at a salary of $50 a week. "Most of them were older than me, but there were a lot of girls in the show 14, 15 years old. I was very unsophisticated," she admits. "I was really just a kid." She rehearsed with other shows, including *Earl Carroll's Vanities*, but "no one could top Ziegfeld." During her stint in the *Follies*, Will Rogers taught her how to spin a rope: "I was the only girl in the show that he would let touch his ropes," she says.

After four years in the company, she jumped at the chance to go on tour. "In order to get the showgirls — I was one of six — to go on the road with *Sally*, we were promised we'd be in *Louie the 14th* with Leon Errol. But I wasn't thinking of that," relates Garvin. "I knew the show was coming to the [West] Coast. I always wanted to be in pictures, and the stage seemed to be the way to get there. Years ago stage people frowned on pictures. Not me — it was something I wanted more than anything in the world.

"They were everything to me — the nickelos, we used to call them. I'd watch the same ones, over and over. Gloria Swanson was my idol. Sometimes I had the nickel, sometimes I didn't. If I couldn't find a nickel and I couldn't sneak in, I'd pick a fight with a boy and beat him up — and they'd let me in. I guess they got a kick out of seeing a girl able to whip a boy."

After leaving Ziegfeld in San Francisco, Garvin made her way to Los Angeles. She found work almost immediately at Christie Studios,

"It's so long ago, it's like another world."

Clowning with Jimmy Finlayson on the Hal Roach lot.

where she made her debut as a chorus girl in a two-reel comedy called *Broadway Lights* (1924). "I never did any extra work there," she says. "The very first picture I did, Al Christie picked me out to do a bit with Bobby Vernon." The comedian flicked a piece of butter on the floor; Anita took a fall and the die was cast.

She was still only 17, but anxious to get ahead: "Christie guaranteed me four days a week. I made quite a few pictures there, but they were just bits. I was there for four months and I couldn't get a lead. I said, 'Mr. Christie, I'm sorry, I'm leaving unless I can do a lead.' He said, 'Don't be silly, Anita, you haven't had enough experience.' I said, 'Sorry, I quit.'"

By the following morning she was working for the Stern Brothers, playing the lead in a picture at Century Studio. She made a number of two-reelers there, with Arthur Lake and others: "Century was quick; you'd make a picture in two, three days."

Director Charles Lamont, with whom she'd worked at Christie, then asked her to join him at Educational Pictures. While there, she co-starred with such popular but now forgotten comedians as Lupino Lane, Lloyd Hamilton, Al St. John and Lige Conley. (The films themselves have been long forgotten.)

Garvin had been in pictures about a year when she found herself working with the up-and-coming Stan Laurel, who had yet to team with Oliver Hardy. When Laurel joined the employ of Hal Roach Studios, he tried to get the comedy pioneer to use Anita in a picture, to no avail. But before long she was appearing in a three-reeler with Mabel Normand (*Raggedy Rose*), under Laurel's direction.

It was at Roach's small, family-like fun factory that Anita's talents would be most fully realized, although she was never under contract. Garvin was cast frequently as Charley Chase's wife or girlfriend, and worked also with such luminaries of the Roach lot as Edgar Kennedy, Thelma Todd and ZaSu Pitts and the Our Gang kids. But it was in the two-reel comedies of Laurel and Hardy that she was seen to best advantage, even in the smallest of parts.

"You know what kills me? *The Battle of the Century*. People remember me in that film, and it was a nothing. "It was *nothing*," she insists (she was also paid nothing). "I was working with Charley [Chase] and Stan came over and said, 'Will you do something for me on your lunch hour? It'll only take a few minutes.'"

At the culmination of the pie fight to end all pie fights, Garvin rounds a corner, slips and falls, and seats herself on a pie. She gets up, determined to retain her dignity, and exits with a dainty wiggle. No less a personage than author Henry Miller called it "the greatest comic film ever made."

As Mrs. Culpepper, with Stan Laurel in *From Soup to Nuts* (1928).

As a stiletto-wielding floozie (*Their Purple Moment*) or a shotgun-toting wife (*Blotto*), her regal countenance and deadpan expression made her the perfect female counterpart for Stan and Ollie. Anita's performance in *From Soup to Nuts*, as the social-climbing Mrs. Culpepper — whose swanky dinner party the team turns into a shambles — is perhaps her crowning achievement. The highlight of the 1928 comedy — and one of the funniest gags Laurel ever devised — is Anita's persistent but futile effort to subdue an elusive cherry that escapes from her fruit cocktail.

A master of the icy glare, Garvin combined devastating facial expressions with an economy of gesture that was rare in silent comedies. Her performances in such films are all the more impressive when one realizes the scenes were usually done in one take: "If you wanted to work, you did it in one take," she says matter-of-factly. "And most everything was off-the-cuff. We'd glance through the script and throw it away."

With Del Henderson and Charley Chase in *Whispering Whoopee* (1930).

Filmmaking was a collaborative art at Roach studios, where the director often had no more authority than the actors. Garvin points to the Charley Chase silent, *Imagine My Embarrassment*, as an example: "We were doing a scene with chewing gum. The director [Hal Yates] was hollering 'Cut, cut, *cut.*' But Charley and I just kept right on going because we found it funny," says Anita. "And every last foot of it was left in the picture.

"One thing about Stan, with apologies to a lot of directors — they thought they were directing him, and they thought they were directing the picture. But Stan was the one," she asserts. "He was very clever about it. The director was never cognizant of the fact that he was not doing all the directing. Even Leo McCarey — and there was no director better. Stan's mind was going all the time; I don't think he had one waking moment when he wasn't thinking of something."

At one point Hal Roach attempted to create a female Laurel and

Hardy by teaming Garvin with actress Marion Byron. The result failed to generate much response and the series was canceled, but not before the pair co-starred with Edgar Kennedy and Stuart Erwin in *A Pair of Tights*. As the recipient of Kennedy's unwelcome advances, her shrewd sense of timing was put to the ultimate test — again under Hal Yates' direction — in this acknowledged masterpiece.

While Garvin appeared in a number of full-length films, her "more demanding" work outside the field of two-reel comedies is all but forgotten. Her features included *The Play Girl* with Madge Bellamy, *Modern Love* with Charley Chase and *The Single Standard* with Greta Garbo. Among the directors who utilized her talents were Alexander Korda (*The Night Watch*), Cecil B. De Mille (*Dynamite*) and Howard Hawks (*Trent's Last Case*).

At Fox Studios, where she did one of her first features (*Bertha, the Sewing Machine Girl*), Garvin was offered a five-year contract in 1927. "I came close to signing, but Actor's Equity had a strike on," she recalls. "Being true to Equity I turned it down; the contract started at $750 and went up to $5,000 in the fifth year, with options. That ruined me at Fox."

Anita turned down more offers than she accepted after marrying bandleader Clifford "Red" Stanley late in 1930, and settling down to raise a family. When her 3-year-old daughter visited her on the set of a Walter Catlett comedy (*Playful Husbands*), Garvin gained a unique insight into the problems of being a working mother — especially a mother working in Hollywood: "The next day I overheard her telling the neighbor, 'I saw Mommy in bed with Walter Catlett.'"

The actress was pregnant with her second child when Leo McCarey — who often requested her services — offered her a prominent part in *Belle of the Nineties* with Mae West. Garvin accepted, but when she discovered the film would take four to six months, she was forced to turn it down.

Garvin returned to the Roach lot, after a long absence, for Laurel and Hardy's *Swiss Miss* (1938). When she became ill after a few days, her role was truncated to a brief but amusing cameo. While she later co-starred with former Ziegfeld cohort Leon Errol in a series of RKO shorts, and worked occasionally with Andy Clyde and the Three Stooges, Garvin decided her place was at home. "I always felt if I was away from the children I was cheating them. I was still just as stagestruck, and wanted a career, but I felt I owed them more than a part-time mother," says Garvin, who retired circa 1943.

The comedienne might have faded into near-total obscurity had it not been for filmmaker Robert Youngson, whose affectionate compilation film, *The Golden Age of Comedy* (1957), reached its

With Kathryn Crawford in Leo McCarey's *Red Hot Rhythm* (1929).

climax with her hilarious plop on-the-pie scene in *The Battle of the Century*. Youngson further spotlighted her talents in *When Comedy Was King* and *Laurel and Hardy's Laughing '20s*, to the delight of a whole new generation.

The Sons of the Desert, an international organization devoted to the memory of Laurel and Hardy, embarked on a dedicated search for the elusive actress, who had vanished seemingly without a trace after her withdrawal from the screen. When she finally surfaced late in 1977 at a meeting of the Way Out West tent — the club's Los Angeles chapter — her presence was duly celebrated. Before she knew it, she was being invited to banquets, film festivals, and other conclaves around the country; in 1982, she was honored by the National Film Society.

When a Disney casting director expressed interest in meeting her, Anita admitted she wouldn't mind going back to work: "the ham in me [started] oinking like mad." She was later approached by an independent producer, but the recent death of her husband — they had

With Greta Garbo in *The Single Standard* (1929).

been married 49 years when Red died suddenly — forced her to reject the offer.

Anita, a great grandmother who lives in Van Nuys, California, enjoys the belated recognition but is still somewhat baffled by all the attention. "I'm very flattered...[but] I feel like a chump. I thought I was ancient history. It's so long ago, it's like another world. A cleaning lady was in my home, she says, 'I know you.' I said, 'No, you don't know me.' She says, '*Laurel and Hardy!*' I get a kick out of it. But it's in another time; you don't relate to it. You know what's fun? It brings back all the old names you've forgotten."

The first interview in 40 years.

THE FILMS OF ANITA GARVIN

Titles are unavailable for most of the many short subjects Garvin made for Christie, Century, Educational, Fox and Joe Rock. She did not appear in THE PAJAMA PARTY (1931), as recorded elsewhere. Film clips of Garvin were used in four compilation features: THE GOLDEN AGE OF COMEDY (1957), WHEN COMEDY WAS KING (1960), LAUREL AND HARDY'S LAUGHING '20s (1965) and THE CRAZY WORLD OF LAUREL AND HARDY (1967).

Shorts

BROADWAY LIGHTS — Christie 1924
THE SNOW HAWK — Standard Cinema-Selznick 1925
THE SLEUTH — Standard Cinema-Selznick 1925
KISS PAPA — Educational 1926
RAGGEDY ROSE — Roach-Pathé 1926
BABY BROTHER — Roach-Pathé 1927
THE OLD WALLOP — Roach-MGM 1927
WITH LOVE AND HISSES — Roach-Pathé 1927
SAILORS BEWARE — Roach-Pathé 1927
HATS OFF — Roach-MGM 1927
THE BATTLE OF THE CENTURY — Roach-MGM 1927
MANY SCRAPPY RETURNS — Roach-Pathé 1927
FORGOTTEN SWEETIES — Roach-Pathé 1927
THE LIGHTER THAT FAILED — Roach-MGM 1927
ASSISTANT WIVES — Roach-Pathé 1927
NEVER THE DAMES SHALL MEET — Roach-MGM 1927
OLD WIVES WHO KNEW — Fox 1928
A PAIR OF TIGHTS — Roach-MGM 1928
FEED 'EM AND WEEP — Roach-MGM 1928
FROM SOUP TO NUTS — Roach-MGM 1928
THEIR PURPLE MOMENT — Roach-MGM 1928
IMAGINE MY EMBARRASSMENT — Roach-MGM 1928
BENDING HUR — Educational 1928 [original title unknown]
OFF TO BUFFALO — Roach-MGM 1929
CRAZY FEET — Roach-MGM 1929
STEPPING OUT — Roach-MGM 1929
ALL STEAMED UP — Fox 1929
THE BIG JEWEL CASE — Educational 1930
WHISPERING WHOOPEE — Roach-MGM 1930
BLOTTO — Roach-MGM 1930
BE BIG — Roach-MGM 1931
LES CAROTTIERS — Roach-MGM 1931 [French version of BE BIG]
LOS CALAVERAS — Roach-MGM 1931 [Spanish version of BE BIG]
THE MILLIONAIRE CAT — RKO Radio 1932
SHOW BUSINESS — Roach-MGM 1932
THE HOLLYWOOD HANDICAP — Universal 1932
YOO HOO — Universal 1932

With Hallam Cooley in *Old Wives Who Knew* (1928).

HIS SILENT RACKET — Roach-MGM 1933
ASLEEP IN THE FEET — Roach-MGM 1933
PLAYFUL HUSBANDS — Columbia 1934
WHILE THE CAT'S AWAY — Vitaphone-Warner Bros. 1936
HOME BONER — RKO Radio 1939
TRUTH ACHES — RKO Radio 1939
COAT TALES — RKO Radio 1939
NOW IT CAN BE SOLD — Columbia 1939
CUCKOO CAVALIERS — Columbia 1940
BESTED BY A BEARD — RKO Radio 1940
HE ASKED FOR IT — RKO Radio 1940
SUNK BY THE CENSUS — RKO Radio 1940

Features

BERTHA, THE SEWING MACHINE GIRL — Fox 1926
THE VALLEY OF HELL — Roach-MGM 1927
THE NIGHT WATCH — First National 1928
THE PLAY GIRL — Fox 1928
THE CHARLATAN — Universal 1929
HER SISTER'S HUSBAND — Tiffany 1929
DYNAMITE — MGM 1929
RED HOT RHYTHM — Pathé 1929
MODERN LOVE — Universal 1929
TRENT'S LAST CASE — Fox 1929
THE SINGLE STANDARD — MGM 1929
SWISS MISS — Roach-MGM 1938
A CHUMP AT OXFORD — Roach-United Artists 1940 *additional scenes for European release*

John Carradine

It took a while to loosen John Carradine's tongue, but once I got the old fox talking he took pleasure in debunking the myths and legends about him that have sprung up over the years. The setting — a makeshift dressing room — was less than ideal. But it afforded me the undeniable privilege of observing him at work, as he did his make up for a dinner theater production. If the play was unmemorable, the interview that preceded it was anything but dull.

Long before John Carradine made a name for himself in Hollywood, he learned there was more to the acting than simply knowing one's craft. John Ford, who gave him some of his finest roles, had a peculiar way of showing appreciation for an actor's talents — in fact, Carradine was sure their association would end even before it began.

Carradine's agent had told him about a role in a script that was floating around town. "He said, 'If they ever do *The Prisoner of Shark Island* there's a part in there that will make you.' I waited two years, and finally Fox decided they were going to do it," recalls the veteran actor, who at 80 is busier than ever.

"I was tested by John Ford, who was going to direct, along with another actor, who did the scene with me. I didn't get on with Ford at all. This was a tough prison sergeant and Ford wanted me to play him like a blithering idiot: drooling at the mouth, slack jaw, vacant eyes. I couldn't see it that way. I tried to play some of the scene the way he wanted it and the rest of it the way I thought it should be played.

"I went back to my dressing room, which I shared with this other actor. I said, 'That's one part I won't get.' He said, 'You've got the part.' I said, 'Oh, no, that baby didn't like me for little sour apples.' He said, 'I'm telling you, you've got the part — he's my brother.' It was Francis Ford. I got the part, and when we did the film I had no problems with Ford at all."

John Ford went on to cast the actor in *Four Men and a Prayer*, *Stagecoach*, *The Grapes of Wrath*, *The Last Hurrah* and other memorable films. Carradine soon found out, however, that the director was a very tricky man. "Ford had an idea an actor couldn't produce the drive he wanted, unless he created a personal animosity between them," asserts Carradine. "I was getting ready to do a scene in *Mary of Scotland*, and Ford was sitting behind me. Suddenly

133

I heard, 'You stupid, lanky, Irish sonuvabitch.' I just about turned around and cold-cocked him.

"Donald Crisp grabbed me and pulled me away and said, 'Don't you know what he's up to?' I said, 'No. The sonuvabitch. What's he up to?' Crisp said, 'He's trying to get you mad, 'cause he thinks he'll get more drive into the scene.' I said, 'Oh, one of those.' I just walked away. Then he called me back to do the scene. We rehearsed it once, he said 'Okay,' and we shot it. No problem. But you had to know how to handle him."

The son of a surgeon mother and a journalist father, Richmond Reed Carradine was born on February 5, 1906, in New York City's Greenwich Village. He was 14 years old when he decided to become an actor, after seeing Robert Bruce Mantell — "then the top Shakespearean actor in the country" — in a production of *The Merchant of Venice*.

He "got sidetracked" in his ambition, however, and ended up as a painter and sculptor after studies at Philadelphia's Graphic Art School. "It kept me going until I began to get somewhere as an actor," he noted. (His father, who died when John was 3, was also a painter, in addition to being a newspaper correspondent of some note).

The young Carradine finally made his acting debut in *Camille* at the St. Charles Theatre in New Orleans in 1925. Three years and a number of odd jobs later — including a stint as a portrait painter at $2.50 a sitting — Carradine drifted into Hollywood, where he found work as a scenic designer for Cecil B. De Mille. "To be a designer you had to be a real architect," he says. "I had studied sculpture, but I couldn't cut it because I wasn't an architect. I lasted two weeks."

Not long after his arrival in Los Angeles, the young actor met one of his idols — John Barrymore, whom he had admired since he was a child. Carradine, who was then rehearsing for the lead in a production of *Richard III*, engineered the meeting himself. Dressed in "the last of my stock wardrobe — striped morning trousers, spats, homburg," he showed up unannounced at Barrymore's residence to ask his advice.

"I didn't crash his estate," says Carradine, contradicting the popular version of the story. "I knocked at what I thought was the front gate and it was the back. I rang the bell and a Japanese voice answered. I said I wanted to see Mr. Barrymore. He didn't say 'What about?' or 'Who are you?' He buzzed the buzzer and I walked in.

"Barrymore appeared in a blue polka dot dressing gown, with his head to one side like a bird. I turned toward him the same way, and he was astonished at this apparition. He took a step toward me and I took a step toward him. He said, 'Dr. Livingston, I presume?' I said, 'Mr. Barrymore, I'm going to play Richard III.' He said, 'Really? Let's have a drink.'

As Rizzio, loyal secretary to *Mary of Scotland* (1936).

"He asked his valet to bring us two Tom Collins. He was very gracious. He spent three-quarters of an hour looking at my script; he said it was as good as any he had seen. Then he said, 'How do you walk as Richard?' I was a little embarrassed to get up and walk like Richard right off the bat, so I went into a long dissertation about it. When I got all through with that, Barrymore looked out over Beverly Hills, and said, 'I walked... like Lionel.'"

Carradine made his film debut as a dim-witted hillbilly in the 1930 remake of *Tol'able David*, at a salary of $100 a week. He asked the director to omit his name from the credits (he was billed as Peter Richmond). A rave review in *Variety* and an offer to play another hillbilly resulted. He turned it down.

The following year — according to Carradine — he was appearing in a play called *Window Panes* with Boris Karloff when he got a call from Universal; a make-up man wanted to make a plaster cast of his face. The make-up test was for the role of the monster in the film version of *Frankenstein* — but when Carradine found out the part had no dialog, he refused it. "I never regretted that I turned it down. Karloff never ceased to be sorry," he claims.

While he accepted a few small movie parts to ward off starvation, he made little effort to compromise or fit in during his early years in Hollywood. "It wasn't contempt," says Carradine. "I just wasn't interested. I was a stage actor, and proud of it. At that time the movies were a kind of bastard art. The first time I did a talking picture we rehearsed it like a play."

Carradine, who got his education in an English-run boarding school, led his early acquaintances in the movie community to believe he was an Englishman. Director James Whale — who cast him in *The Bride of Frankenstein* — thought the actor was one of his native countrymen. "So many people thought I was British in those days, I just let it go at that," notes Carradine. "Basil Rathbone was a close friend of mine who for years thought I was British."

The tall, thin actor's affected manner, together with his decidedly offbeat appearance, gained him a reputation as an eccentric in his early days — an image he disputes today. "I was accused of wearing a cape, walking up and down Hollywood Boulevard. That isn't true," he states. "I didn't have a cape. I had an overcoat that was given to me by a friend who was short and fat. The sleeves were too short, so I couldn't wear it; I wore it over my shoulders, and it looked like a cape — so I got a reputation for wearing one.

"The stories about me reciting Shakespeare on Hollywood Boulevard are a legend that has no basis in fact," he insists. "But I did do it in the Hollywood Bowl, every night at midnight for five years. Bellowed

Shakespeare at 20,000 empty seats. I did it to strengthen my voice. I wasn't eccentric; I was just trying to learn my craft, and improve what I had."

The six-year contract Carradine signed with 20th Century-Fox in 1936 made him one of the busiest actors in Hollywood (he did 39 pictures for Fox alone over the next six years; his favorite film — *Captains Courageous* — was a 26-week loan-out to MGM.)

The document also robbed the bohemian actor of a treasured possession — his freedom. "In those days, you did what you were told. If you refused a part, they put you on suspension. There was a part they gave me I didn't want to do, but I was raising a family. I couldn't afford to go on suspension," says Carradine, who was then married to Ardanelle McCool Cosner (the first of four wives) and already had two children.

"Another actor took the suspension. He was getting the same

With Claud Allister in *Captain Fury* (1939).

With Warner Baxter in *Kidnapped* (1938).

thing I was, $300 a week. His name was Anthony Quinn. Three weeks later they brought him back, gave him $1,000 a week. That was what he wanted. But I'd signed a contract; I gave them my word and that was it. I've never broken a contract, and never will. I didn't get that much [$1,000 a week] for five years."

In addition to John Ford, directors like Cecil B. De Mille (*The Crusades*), Richard Boleslawski (*Les Miserables*) and Henry King (*Jesse James*) called on Carradine repeatedly. Regardless of how well he got to know them, however, the actor could never second guess some of his directors — especially Ford.

"He was an odd man to work for. If you suggested something you wanted to do that hadn't been rehearsed, he'd give you that cold fisheye and say, 'You want to direct the rest of the picture?' Or he'd

With Henry Fonda and John Qualen in *The Grapes of Wrath* (1940).

announce to the company, 'Mr. Carradine will direct this scene.'

"I had a scene in *The Grapes of Wrath* with Henry Fonda, and I had an idea. Preacher Casy was talking about a preacher who took a running jump over a fence to illustrate a sermon. I wanted to jump over, and trip and fall. I didn't dare suggest it to Ford," says Carradine, whose impassioned portrayal of Casy is generally considered his best. "So I took Hank Fonda aside and told him quietly. Ford said, 'What was that?' I said, 'Oh, you wouldn't be interested.' He said, 'Yes, I would.' Finally I told him. He chewed on his handkerchief a moment, and he said, 'Yeah, do it.'"

Richard Boleslawski was tough on him but "Boleslawski was an artist," says Carradine, "and I respected him. He was a big, lovable bear of a man. David Selznick came on the set of *The Garden of Allah* and bawled him out in front of the whole company. I thought that was a lousy thing for Selznick to do; Boleslawski was a great director and everybody loved him."

Carradine returned to the stage as Louis XI in the 1941 Los Angeles and San Francisco productions of *The Vagabond King*. Two years later, under the aegis of his own Shakespearean repertory company, he produced, directed and starred in *Hamlet, The Merchant of Venice*, and *Othello* (in which he alternated between Othello and Iago).

The actor, who reportedly mortgaged his home to finance the tour, failed in his ambition of becoming "the pre-eminent Shakespearean actor of my day." But his endeavor was triumphant: the troupe played up and down the West Coast to sellout crowds.

Though he never took the Bard to Broadway, Carradine appeared frequently on the New York stage in the years immediately after the war. He stretched his acting muscles and quenched his thirst for the theater with such disparate roles as the Cardinal in *The Duchess of Malfi*, the Inquisitor in Brecht's *Galileo*, and the Ragpicker in *The Madwoman of Chaillot*.

The price of such freedom did not come cheap, however. In order to finance his love affair with the stage, Carradine began to accept all manner of film offers, regardless of quality. Beginning with *Captive Wild Woman* in 1943, he did a slew of low-budget horror films at Universal and Monogram. Throughout the 1940s, he typically played either the mad doctor (*Revenge of the Zombies*) or the victim of deranged experiments by others (*Voodoo Man*); he also turned up as a debonair Count Dracula in *House of Dracula*. In between he won roles in classier material, including the garrulous Bret Harte in *The Adventures of Mark Twain*, and the crooked lawyer trying to cheat Fred Allen in *It's in the Bag*.

When work in feature films began to dry up in the 1950s, Carradine busied himself with television. He appeared regularly in such series as *Lights Out*, *Climax*, *Bat Masterson*, *Thriller* and *The Red Skelton Show*, in addition to showcases like *Playhouse 90*.

He returned to Broadway as Kit Carson in the 1955 revival of *The Time of Your Life*. Seven years later, he co-starred opposite Zero Mostel in *A Funny Thing Happened on the Way to the Forum*. As Marcus Lycus, Carradine enjoyed a six-month Broadway run in the zany musical, followed by a hugely successful tour.

While Carradine rightly claims to have played in "some of the greatest pictures ever made," he readily acknowledges his appearance in some of the worst. "I've done a lot of crap," he admits. "I started doing it when I was under contract at Fox. I only did 'em for the money. I had five boys to raise."

But the actor contends that he has has also turned down his share of such films. "Once I was supposed to go to the producer's office to sign a contract," he says. "I'd read the first three pages of the script and it was awful. I called him up, by virtue of having had four scotches with Mickey Rooney. I said, 'I'm not going to be in your office at 3 o'clock, I'm not going to sign the contract; I'm not going to do the picture.' He said, 'Good God, why not?' I said, 'I've learned I cannot read lines and vomit at the same time.'"

Carradine, who singles out *Billy the Kid vs. Dracula* (1966) as the worst of his pictures — "an awful piece of crap" — has amassed a long list of undistinguished film credits in the past two decades. But along

As Bret Harte in *The Adventures of Mark Twain* (1944).

with such feeble efforts as *Horror of the Blood Monsters*, he has also been seen in more stylish examples of the genre, like *The Howling*.

Rare departures into mainstream cinema have included Woody Allen's *Everything You Always Wanted to Know About Sex*, in a parody of his mad doctor roles; *The Shootist* with John Wayne; the animated feature, *The Secret of NIMH*; and more recently, Francis Ford Coppola's *Peggy Sue Got Married*. The actor, who vows he'll never retire, recently won an Emmy for his performance in the children's special, *Umbrella Jack*. He completed work on his 500th feature film (by his count) — *The Revenge* — in the spring of 1986. He and his manager, Robert Byron, have their own production company; Carraby has several films awaiting release, and more on tap.

Carradine, who lives in San Diego, California, and is writing his memoirs, spends much of his time on stage these days. Gaunt as ever, his face is creased with age and his hands disfigured by arthritis. But the actor's enthusiasm for his work, and his powerful voice, are boundless and undiminished.

He has played theaters large and small across the country in recent years, as Sir Thomas More in *A Man For All Seasons* (his favorite role), Norman Thayer in *On Golden Pond*, and Jeeter Lester in *Tobacco Road*. In 1977 he played Big Daddy in *Cat on a Hot Tin Roof* — a role he was forced to turn down in the original production, due to prior commitments.

Though he can still be tempted by Broadway — he played the blind hermit in a production of *Frankenstein* (1981) that closed in one night — he prefers the college circuit. "Broadway theater is just as crassly commercial as pictures," he asserts. "That's why I work a lot in colleges. I do what I want to do, and I have a ball. College kids are so anxious to learn and so full of enthusiasm — they're fun to work with."

Not surprisingly, his advice to aspiring young actors is "go to college and major in English literature. Stay away from acting schools; they're run by people who couldn't make it in the theater," he says. "Acting is an art about which there's a great deal to be learned and nothing which can be taught. You have to learn by doing."

While he encouraged sons David, Keith and Robert to become actors, and directed all of them in stage productions, he also advised them to develop their own style. "So they did — and they're doing fine. None of them turned out like me," says the proud patriarch of the Carradine clan. "They've got their own style."

"What the critics have to say doesn't affect me at all."

THE FILMS OF JOHN CARRADINE

Carradine was billed as John Peter Richmond from 1930-34, appearing under his own name from 1935 on. He did not appear in OF HUMAN BONDAGE (1934), KING OF THE ZOMBIES (1941), THE BLACK SWAN (1942) or HOT SPOT (1973), as recorded elsewhere; he was slated for but did not appear in THE LONG RIDERS (1980). Film clips of Carradine were included in two documentaries, DIRECTED BY JOHN FORD (1971) and THE SPENCER TRACY LEGACY (1986). Some TV specials in which Carradine appeared, such as GREATEST HEROES OF THE BIBLE (1978), have been incorrectly listed as TV movies in certain references. Titles are unavailable for many of the low budget horror films Carradine has made in recent years. Based on a list compiled by Jim Beaver, and other sources.

Shorts

INFORMATION PLEASE (No. 5) — RKO Radio 1942
SOMETHING FOR MRS. GIBBS — Van Praag Productions 1965 [industrial]
THRESHOLD — J. Maynard Louins 1970
SHADOW HOUSE — American Film Institute 1972
THE LEGEND OF SLEEPY HOLLOW — Bosustow 1972 *narrator*

Features

TOL'ABLE DAVID — Columbia 1930
BRIGHT LIGHTS — First National 1930
HEAVEN ON EARTH — Universal 1931
FORGOTTEN COMMANDMENTS — Paramount 1932
THE SIGN OF THE CROSS — Paramount 1932
THE STORY OF TEMPLE DRAKE — Paramount 1933
THIS DAY AND AGE — Paramount 1933
TO THE LAST MAN (Law of Vengeance) — Paramount 1933
THE INVISIBLE MAN — Universal 1933
THE BLACK CAT — Universal 1934
CLEOPATRA — Paramount 1934
THE MEANEST GAL IN TOWN — RKO Radio 1934
CLIVE OF INDIA — United Artists 1935
TRANSIENT LADY — Universal 1935
CARDINAL RICHELIEU — United Artists 1935
LES MISERABLES — United Artists 1935
BRIDE OF FRANKENSTEIN — Universal 1935
ALIAS MARY DOW — Universal 1935
THE CRUSADES — Paramount 1935 *voice*
SHE GETS HER MAN — Universal 1935
BAD BOY — Fox 1935
THE MAN WHO BROKE THE BANK AT MONTE CARLO — Fox 1935
ANYTHING GOES (Tops Is The Limit) — Paramount 1936

THE PRISONER OF SHARK ISLAND — 20th Century-Fox 1936
A MESSAGE TO GARCIA — 20th Century-Fox 1936 *voice*
CAPTAIN JANUARY — 20th Century-Fox 1936 *scenes deleted*
UNDER TWO FLAGS — 20th Century-Fox 1936
HALF ANGEL — 20th Century-Fox 1936 *voice*
WHITE FANG — 20th Century-Fox 1936
MARY OF SCOTLAND — RKO Radio 1936
RAMONA — 20th Century-Fox 1936
DIMPLES — 20th Century-Fox 1936
DANIEL BOONE — RKO Radio 1936
THE GARDEN OF ALLAH — Selznick-United Artists 1936
WINTERSET — RKO Radio 1936
LAUGHING AT TROUBLE (Laughing at Death) — 20th Century-Fox 1936
NANCY STEELE IS MISSING — 20th Century-Fox 1937
CAPTAINS COURAGEOUS — MGM 1937
THIS IS MY AFFAIR — 20th Century-Fox 1937
LOVE UNDER FIRE — 20th Century-Fox 1937
ALI BABA GOES TO TOWN — 20th Century-Fox 1937
THE HURRICANE — Goldwyn-United Artists 1937
THE LAST GANGSTER — MGM 1937
DANGER! LOVE AT WORK — 20th Century-Fox 1937
THANK YOU, MR. MOTO — 20th Century-Fox 1937
INTERNATIONAL SETTLEMENT — 20th Century-Fox 1938
OF HUMAN HEARTS — MGM 1938
FOUR MEN AND A PRAYER — 20th Century-Fox 1938
KENTUCKY MOONSHINE — 20th Century-Fox 1938
KIDNAPPED — 20th Century-Fox 1938
I'LL GIVE A MILLION — 20th Century-Fox 1938
ALEXANDER'S RAGTIME BAND — 20th Century-Fox 1938
GATEWAY — 20th Century-Fox 1938
SUBMARINE PATROL — 20th Century-Fox 1938
JESSE JAMES — 20th Century-Fox 1939
MR. MOTO'S LAST WARNING — 20th Century-Fox 1939
THE THREE MUSKETEERS — 20th Century-Fox 1939
STAGECOACH — United Artists 1939
THE HOUND OF THE BASKERVILLES — 20th Century-Fox 1939
CAPTAIN FURY — Roach-United Artists 1939
FIVE CAME BACK — RKO Radio 1939
FRONTIER MARSHAL — 20th Century-Fox 1939
DRUMS ALONG THE MOHAWK — 20th Century-Fox 1939
THE GRAPES OF WRATH — 20th Century-Fox 1940
THE RETURN OF FRANK JAMES — 20th Century-Fox 1940
BRIGHAM YOUNG — FRONTIERSMAN — 20th Century-Fox 1940
CHAD HANNA — 20th Century-Fox 1940
WESTERN UNION — 20th Century-Fox 1941
BLOOD AND SAND — 20th Century-Fox 1941
MAN HUNT — 20th Century-Fox 1941
SWAMP WATER — 20th Century-Fox 1941

ALL THAT MONEY CAN BUY (The Devil and Daniel Webster, Here Is a
    Man) — RKO Radio 1941 *extra*
SON OF FURY — 20th Century-Fox 1942
WHISPERING GHOSTS — 20th Century-Fox 1942
NORTHWEST RANGERS — MGM 1942
REUNION IN FRANCE — MGM 1942
I ESCAPED FROM THE GESTAPO (No Escape) — Monogram 1943
CAPTIVE WILD WOMAN — Universal 1943
HITLER'S MADMAN (Hitler's Hangman) — PRC-MGM 1943
SILVER SPURS — Republic 1943
ISLE OF FORGOTTEN SINS (Monsoon) — PRC 1943
GANGWAY FOR TOMORROW — RKO Radio 1943
REVENGE OF THE ZOMBIES — Monogram 1943
WATERFRONT — PRC 1944
VOODOO MAN — Monogram 1944
THE BLACK PARACHUTE — Columbia 1944
THE ADVENTURES OF MARK TWAIN — Warner Bros. 1944
THE INVISIBLE MAN'S REVENGE — Universal 1944
JUNGLE WOMAN — Universal 1944 [stock footage
    from CAPTIVE WILD WOMAN]
RETURN OF THE APE MAN — Monogram 1944
THE MUMMY'S GHOST — Universal 1944
BARBARY COAST GENT — MGM 1944
BLUEBEARD — PRC 1944
ALASKA — Monogram 1944
HOUSE OF FRANKENSTEIN — Universal 1944
IT'S IN THE BAG — United Artists 1945
CAPTAIN KIDD — United Artists 1945
HOUSE OF DRACULA — Universal 1945
FALLEN ANGEL — 20th Century-Fox 1945
FACE OF MARBLE — Monogram 1946
DOWN MISSOURI WAY — PRC 1946
THE PRIVATE AFFAIRS OF BEL AMI — United Artists 1947
C-MAN — Film Classics 1949
CASANOVA'S BIG NIGHT — Paramount 1954
THUNDER PASS — Lippert 1954
JOHNNY GUITAR — Republic 1954
THE EGYPTIAN — 20th Century-Fox 1954
STRANGER ON HORSEBACK — United Artists 1955
THE KENTUCKIAN — United Artists 1955
DESERT SANDS — United Artists 1955
HIDDEN GUNS — Republic 1956
THE COURT JESTER — Paramount 1956
FEMALE JUNGLE — ARC-American International Pictures 1956
THE BLACK SLEEP (Dr. Cadman's Secret) — United Artists 1956
AROUND THE WORLD IN 80 DAYS — Todd-United Artists 1956
THE TEN COMMANDMENTS — Paramount 1956
DARK VENTURE — 1st National — 1956

With David Niven in *Four Men and a Prayer* (1938).

THE TRUE STORY OF JESSE JAMES — 20th Century-Fox 1957
THE UNEARTHLY — Republic 1957
THE STORY OF MANKIND — Warner Bros. 1957
HELL SHIP MUTINY — Republic 1957
HALF HUMAN (Jujin Yukiotoko) — Toho-DCA 1957 *additional scenes for U.S. release*
THE PROUD REBEL — Buena Vista 1958
SHOWDOWN AT BOOT HILL — 20th Century-Fox 1958
THE LAST HURRAH — Columbia 1958
THE COSMIC MAN — Allied Artists 1959
INVISIBLE INVADERS — United Artists 1959
THE OREGON TRAIL — 20th Century-Fox 1959
THE INCREDIBLE PETRIFIED WORLD — Governor 1960 [filmed 1958]
TARZAN THE MAGNIFICENT — Paramount 1960
THE ADVENTURES OF HUCKLEBERRY FINN — MGM 1960
SEX KITTENS GO TO COLLEGE (The Beauty and the Robot) — Allied Artists 1960
INVASION OF THE ANIMAL PEOPLE — ADP 1962 [filmed 1958] *additional scenes for U.S. release*
THE MAN WHO SHOT LIBERTY VALANCE — Paramount 1962
THE PATSY — Paramount 1964
CHEYENNE AUTUMN — Warner Bros. 1964
CURSE OF THE STONE HAND — ADP 1964 *additional scenes for U.S. release*
THE WIZARD OF MARS — American General 1964
HOUSE OF THE BLACK DEATH — Taurus 1966
MUNSTER, GO HOME — Universal 1966
BILLY THE KID VS. DRACULA — Embassy 1966
BROKEN SABRE — Paramount 1966 [comprised of *Branded* TV episodes; no U.S. theatrical release]
NIGHT TRAIN TO MUNDO FINE — Hollywood Star 1966
THE FIEND WITH THE ELECTRONIC BRAIN (Psycho A Go-Go!, Blood of Ghastly Horror, Man With the Synthetic Brain) — Independent International 1966 *additional scenes for U.S. release*
THE EMPEROR'S NEW CLOTHES — Cue 1966 [no theatrical release]
HILLBILLYS IN A HAUNTED HOUSE — Woolner Brothers 1967
DR. TERROR'S GALLERY OF HORRORS (The Blood Suckers, Return From the Past) — American General 1967
LA SENORA MUERTE (The Death Woman) — Columbia 1967
THE HOSTAGE — Crown International 1968
PACTO DIABOLICO (Diabolical Pact; Pact With the Devil) — Luis Vergara 1968
THEY RAN FOR THEIR LIVES — Color Vision International 1968
THE ASTRO-ZOMBIES — Geneni 1968
AUTOPSIA DE UN FANTASMA (Autopsy of a Ghost) — Peliculas Nacionales 1968
THE HELICOPTER SPIES — MGM 1968 [comprised of *Man From UNCLE* TV episodes; no U.S. theatrical release]

With Woody Allen in *Everything You Always Wanted to Know About Sex* (1972).

GENESIS — Filmways-General Film Distributors 1968 [compilation of
   student films] *narrator*
BLOOD OF DRACULA'S CASTLE — Crown International 1969
THE GOOD GUYS AND THE BAD GUYS — Warner Bros.-
   Seven Arts 1969
THE TROUBLE WITH GIRLS — MGM 1969
DAUGHTER OF THE MIND — 20th Century-Fox-ABC 1969 [TV movie]
LAS VAMPIRAS (The Vampires) — Columbia 1969
CAIN'S CUTTHROATS (Cain's Way, Justice Cain) — MDA Associates 1970
HELL'S BLOODY DEVILS (The Fakers, Smashing the Crime Syndicate,
   Swastika Savages, Operation M) — Independent International 1970
CROWHAVEN FARM — Aaron Spelling-ABC 1970 [TV movie]
BLOOD OF THE IRON MAIDEN (Trip to Terror, Is This Trip Really
   Necessary?) —Hollywood Star 1970
THE McMASTERS — Chevron 1970
MYRA BRECKINRIDGE — 20th Century-Fox 1970
HORROR OF THE BLOOD MONSTERS (Vampire Men of the Lost Planet)
   — Independent International 1970
FIVE BLOODY GRAVES (Gun Riders) — Independent International 1970
SHINBONE ALLEY — Allied Artists 1971 *voice*
THE SEVEN MINUTES — 20th Century-Fox 1971

BIGFOOT — Western International-Ellman Enterprises 1971
DECISIONS! DECISIONS! — NBC 1972 [TV movie]
BOXCAR BERTHA — American International Pictures 1972
PORTNOY'S COMPLAINT — Warner Bros. 1972 *voice*
EVERYTHING YOU ALWAYS WANTED TO KNOW ABOUT SEX* (*BUT
   WERE AFRAID TO ASK) — United Artists 1972
THE GATLING GUN (King Gun) — Universal Entertainment-Ellman
   Enterprises 1972
RICHARD — Aurora City Group 1972
MOON CHILD — American Films-Filmmakers Ltd. 1972
THRESHOLD 9 ILLUSIONS — 1972 [never completed]
THE NIGHT STRANGLER — ABC Circle 1973 [TV movie]
LEGACY OF BLOOD — Ellman Enterprises 1973
TERROR IN THE WAX MUSEUM — Cinerama 1973
BAD CHARLESTON CHARLIE — International Cinema 1973
SUPERCHICK — Crown International 1973
HEX (Grass Land) — 20th Century-Fox 1973
1,000,000 A.D. — Cine-Fund 1973 [no theatrical release]
SILENT NIGHT, BLOODY NIGHT (Zora, Death House, Night of the Full
   Dark Moon) — Cannon Releasing 1973
HOUSE OF THE SEVEN CORPSES — International Amusement Corp.-
   Television Corp. of America 1974
THE CAT CREATURE — Screen Gems-Columbia-ABC 1973 [TV movie]
MARY, MARY, BLOODY MARY — Translor 1975
STOWAWAY TO THE MOON — 20th Century-Fox-CBS 1975 [TV movie]
WON TON TON, THE DOG WHO SAVED HOLLYWOOD —
   Paramount 1976
THE KILLER INSIDE ME — Warner Bros. 1976
THE SHOOTIST — Paramount 1976
THE LAST TYCOON — Paramount 1976
DEATH AT LOVE HOUSE — (The Shrine of Lorna Love) — Spelling-
   Goldberg-ABC 1976 [TV movie]
CRASH — Group I 1976
CAPTAINS AND THE KINGS — Universal-NBC 1976 [TV movie]
THE LADY AND THE LYNCHINGS — Secondari-PBS 1977 [TV movie]
THE SENTINEL — Universal 1977
THE WHITE BUFFALO (Hunt to Kill) — United Artists 1977
SATAN'S CHEERLEADERS — World Amusements 1977
TAIL GUNNER JOE — Universal-NBC 1977 [TV movie]
JOURNEY INTO THE BEYOND — Burbank International 1977 *narrator*
SHOCK WAVES (Death Corps) — Joseph Brenner Productions 1977
GOLDEN RENDEZVOUS — Film Trust 1977
CHRISTMAS MIRACLE IN CAUFIELD, U.S.A. (The Christmas Coal Mine
   Miracle) — 20th Century-Fox-NBC 1977 [TV movie]
VAMPIRE HOOKERS — Caprican Three 1978
SUNSET COVE (Save Our Beach) — Cal-Am Artists 1978
THE BEES (Buzzz) — New World 1978
MONSTER: THE LEGEND THAT BECAME A TERROR (Monsteroid) —
   Academy International 1979 [filmed 1977]

THE SEEKERS — Operation Prime Time-Universal-HBO 1979 [TV movie]
TEHERAN INCIDENT (Missile X, The Neutron Bomb Incident, Cruise
    Missile) — Omnia 1979
NOCTURNA (Granddaughter of Dracula) — Compass International 1979
AMERICATHON — Lorimar-United Artists 1979 *scenes deleted*
THE MANDATE OF HEAVEN — White Bread Productions 1979
THE CARRADINES IN CONCERT — Alfie Productions 1979 [documentary]
THE BOOGEYMAN — Jerry Gross Organization 1980
THE MONSTER CLUB — ITC Film Distributors 1981
    [no U.S. theatrical release]
THE HOWLING — Avco Embassy 1981
THE NESTING (Phobia) — Feature Films 1981 [filmed 1979] *also narrator*
GOLIATH AWAITS — Operation Prime Time-Columbia 1981 [TV movie]
ZORRO, THE GAY BLADE — 20th Century-Fox 1981 *scenes deleted*
FRANKENSTEIN ISLAND — Jerry Warren 1981
SATAN'S MISTRESS (Demon Rage, Dark Eyes, Fury of the Succubus) —
    Diversified Film Productions-MPM 1982
THE SECRET OF NIMH — Don Bluth-MGM-United Artists 1982 *voice*
BOOGEYMAN II — New West Films 1983 [stock footage
    from THE BOOGEYMAN; no theatrical release]
KLYNHAM SUMMER (The Scarecrow) — Oasis Films Limited 1983
HOUSE OF THE LONG SHADOWS — Cannon Releasing 1983
EVILS OF THE NIGHT — Aquarius Releasing 1983†
MONSTER IN THE CLOSET — Troma 1983†
THE IMMORAL MINORITY PICTURE SHOW (IMPS) — Scott
    Mansfield 1983†
THE ICE PIRATES — MGM-United Artists 1984
THE VALS — Entertainment Artists 1985
THE TOMB — Fred Olen Ray 1985 [working title] †
PEGGY SUE GOT MARRIED — Tri-Star 1986‡
BOOGEYMAN III — 1986‡
CAPTAIN WILLOUGHBY — Carraby 1986‡
BIGFOOT — Carraby 1986 [documentary] ‡
THE HERMIT — Carraby-Showtime 1986 [TV movie] ‡
SECRETS OF DR. TAVANER — New Heights 1986‡
THE ICE KING — Kraft Films 1986‡
THE REVENGE — United Productions 1986‡
WALDEN'S POND — Carraby 1986 [documentary] ‡

†*Unreleased productions slated for release during 1986-87.*
‡*Recent productions slated for release during 1986-87.*

Rolfe Sedan

Rolfe Sedan might have been embarrassed by his inclusion in the cast of characters assembled for this volume, but I feel he is worthy of recognition. He may be more obscure than the others, but he's a star in my book — warm, gracious, witty, personable — a fine actor, and a treasured friend. He was doubtful when I encouraged him to make public appearances; his reluctance gave way when he was unexpectedly beseiged by fans and admirers.

Although he once got star billing in the theater, he found himself reduced to the rank of bit player in the movies. His career, which spanned seven decades, earned him neither fame nor fortune. But the late Rolfe Sedan had one thing money couldn't buy: respect.

"I've never played the game, the social game you have to play," the actor conceded, toward the end of his career. "And I refuse to beg. There's something that doesn't allow me to be subservient to somebody to get a job. It isn't in my make-up. These comics who play Las Vegas, they all play the game; they have to. Same thing in pictures — if you know where the body is buried, then you get the parts.

"I've spent my whole life playing chefs, waiters, valets and clerks," observed Sedan, who was seen as Mr. Beasley, the mailman, on *The George Burns and Gracie Allen Show*, and later played the train conductor in Mel Brooks' *Young Frankenstein.* "I've had a whole career in pictures making something out of nothing, always hoping for a break. I lost out; I should've been on top of the heap."

Born January 20, 1896 in New York, Edward Sedan was the son of a Broadway couturiere and a symphony conductor. (His father, Alexander, played bit parts in silent films between engagements with the symphony.) After studying to be a scientific agriculturist, the younger Sedan decided "it wasn't in my blood." He also worked as a paymaster for a construction company before turning his energies to the theater.

"There was never a point where I decided to go on stage. Being surrounded by music and art and theater I just drifted into it as a natural thing; I saw it happening and I wanted to be a part of it," he said. "At first I was a dancer. But I was versatile — I could do 16 dialects, sing if necessary. Nothing stopped me in my younger days; I did everything.

"When I was 12 years old, I went to this theater where Anna Held was doing a show. I went backstage and asked the manager if there was any work. He said, 'You wanna lead a donkey across the stage?' I said, 'Sure.' That was my debut."

The Follies of the Day (1914) — in which he portrayed George M. Cohan — was one of the highlights of Sedan's early years in show business. He went on to understudy Al Jolson in *The Passing Show of 1916*, then traveled with different vaudeville acts as a song-and-dance man. When he failed to find a suitable partner, he entered burlesque as a dialectician. Light opera followed, and a series of comedy leads.

Rolfe started in films as an adolescent, doing extra work for such pioneer East Coast companies as Vitagraph, Yankee, Thanhouser and Kalem. "They came down to the school — they wanted some kids, for $2 or $3 a day. If the film busted," he recalled, "you had to stay in that position until the guy went and reloaded the camera. It was a lark — we did it to have some money in our pockets."

Sedan made his official debut in a now forgotten all-star film of 1919, headlined by Noah Beery Sr. Two years later, the actor was appearing in *The Firefly* with Lawrence Tibbett, at the Mason Opera House in Los Angeles; a scout from Universal spotted him, and put him under contract.

The studio cast Rolfe in one picture after another, features as well

Barbering, with Clara Bow and Ernest Torrence in *Man Trap* (1926).

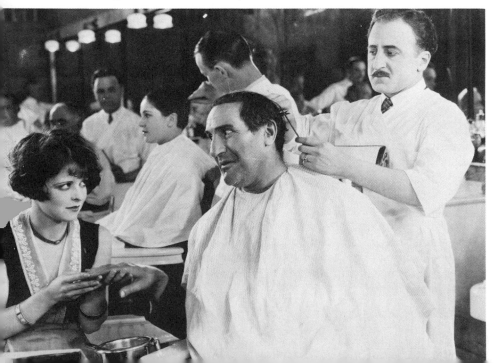

as shorts. "I played in everything there," he said. "I was a Frenchman, a German, an Italian... directors were forced to take me because I got paid whether I worked or not."

After four years at Universal — and a succession of silent films with Laura La Plante, Hoot Gibson and Lon Chaney Sr. — Sedan began to freelance. At MGM, he played a waiter in Erich von Stroheim's version of *The Merry Widow*; at Paramount, he appeared in the original *Beau Geste*. Director Harry Pollard, who had taken a liking to the young actor, brought him back to Universal for the role of an effeminate valet, in *Uncle Tom's Cabin* (1927).

"They thought I was the man for it — I had to dance, do the cakewalk and stuff — so I blacked up and they put my hair in little curls. I worked six months on that picture, and the rest of the cast never knew I was white," mused Sedan. "You did things like that back then. In westerns they shot real bullets at you — what the hell, they could kill you! — we never gave it a thought in those days. They'd throw you off a boat; nobody asked if you could swim."

Sedan's talents were often put to work at the Hal Roach Studios, where he never knew what would come up in the course of the day. One morning he was playing a hotel desk clerk in a Laurel and Hardy comedy (*Double Whoopee*), when an eager lass named Jean Harlow stepped before him — revealing nearly all of her endearing young charms.

With Sammy Blum and Almeda Fowler in *Party Girl* (1930).

With Leo White (left), Patsy Kelly, Eddie Conrad and Thelma Todd in *Done in Oil* (1934).

"We weren't told she was going to come in naked," exclaimed Rolfe. "There was no rehearsal or anything. And all of a sudden, down she comes, walking the entire length of the hotel lobby. I had no idea she was going to walk up to me! She was standing there with almost nothing on. Her mother was there; she thought nothing of it. Even though I'd been in burlesque, they didn't walk around *like that*." (An alternate take, with Harlow only slightly more modest in costume, was used in the film).

Sedan also worked with Harold Lloyd on the Roach lot, but found the experience less than pleasant: "The entire time I just sat there — he wouldn't let me play the part. It was too much competition. Lloyd said, 'I can't allow anybody to top me.' The same thing happened with Ginger Rogers on *Lux Radio Theatre*. She wouldn't come to the microphone with me; she said I drew too much attention.

"You have to be careful with comedy, especially now. It depends on who you work with — if you're too funny, you don't play again. Today, you can't get a laugh if it isn't in the script," lamented Sedan. "They don't hire you to get laughs anymore, they hire you to feed them to the stars. Back then, actors played off each other. If you could get a laugh, by all means get it — as long as you didn't kill the other guy's."

Rolfe appeared in perhaps 300 films, often delivering no more than a single line of dialog and sometimes none at all. In *The Iron Mask* (1929), opposite Douglas Fairbanks, he had an unusually prominent part as the foppish Louis XIII — a role that required him to wear expensive wigs and costumes.

In *Ruggles of Red Gap*, he was the barber who trimmed Charlie Ruggles' mustache, and had his own clipped in retaliation; in *A Night at the Opera*, he was a bearded Russian aviator who lost his uniform — and his whiskers — to the Marx Brothers. He was a taxi driver in *Love Me Tonight*, a ballet master in *Shall We Dance*, a croupier in *Topper Takes a Trip*, a balloon mechanic in *The Wizard of Oz* and a theatrical producer in *The Story of Vernon and Irene Castle*.

Sedan's favorite, of all his films, was *Bluebeard's Eighth Wife* (1938), wherein he had a memorable altercation in a department store with Gary Cooper, who wanted to buy only the top half of a pair of pajamas. Initially cast as a salesclerk, Sedan was recommended for the role of the floorwalker when another actor couldn't play the part to director Ernst Lubitsch's satisfaction.

The crew adjourned for the day while Rolfe nervously studied his new lines. He returned the next morning to find Lubitsch fighting for him, trying to keep him despite studio disapproval. Once they reached an agreement, they were in such a hurry to make up for lost time they tried to rush him through the scene.

"Gary Cooper came over to me and he said, 'Look kid, I'm with you. Don't worry; take your time.' I went back and studied the part. We walked through it once and Lubitsch said, 'All right, we'll do it.' We started out and I went blank. A second time, blank.

"Lubitsch was getting angry," he recalled. "I could hear them calling agents, trying to get another actor. I said, 'Look, Mr. Lubitsch, I want to have a rehearsal with nobody on this set. Everybody off the set, the camera off the set; I want to do it my way.' He looked at me and he said, 'All right, you want it that way — you've got it.' I rehearsed twice with Cooper. He didn't say a word, Gary, he just patted me on the back. He knew what I was going through. I said, 'Okay, now I'm ready.' And we did it.

"The executives were *burning*. Lubitsch was fired off the lot after that," claimed Sedan, "and I didn't work at Paramount for years. It

As Mr. Beasley, with Gracie Allen.

was unheard of — nobody knew who I was, and I was telling 150 people to get off the set. But Lubitsch stuck with me; he understood my position. And later he called me to play the hotel manager in *Ninotchka*.

"Lubitsch was a wonderful man to work for," said Sedan, who was in at least eight of the director's films. "He was a comic himself — he could see if a man had the comedy material. A lot of directors feel superior to everybody on the set; they have no patience with people. Josef von Sternberg would walk around with a stick and hit people on the ankles. I worked with Orson Welles on the New York stage — that man was impossible. He had no sympathy with the small man."

Frustrated by the size of his roles, Sedan left Hollywood in 1941 to try his luck again in New York. He appeared in a number of stage productions during a four-year hiatus from films, including *All Men Are Alike* and Moliere's *The Would-Be Gentleman*, both with comedian Bobby Clark.

Late in 1944, he auditioned for the Broadway production of *A Bell for Adano*, starring Fredric March. Rolfe — who had become typecast as a Frenchman in Hollywood — tried out for the role of Nasta, the

Fascist mayor, and won out over a group of genuine Italian actors.

Sedan was busier in radio than most film actors. He was heard on such programs as *The Saint* and *I Love a Mystery*, and was a regular on *The Joe Penner Show*. *The Smilin' Ed McConnell Show*, a kiddie program he did on both radio and television, made use of his talent for dialects.

Rolfe was even more active on TV, where he turned up on *Superman*, *The Gale Storm Show*, *The Jack Benny Show*, *The Addams Family*, *Maude* and dozens of others. The recurring role of the befuddled postman on *Burns and Allen* — still seen in reruns — remains one of his more memorable.

"I had to audition five times to get that part," observed Sedan. "Finally the guys up on the catwalk, the electricians, they laughed — so George Burns figured I was the one for the job. Then Jack Benny got an idea — I should be the mailman on his show too, bringing the dirt from one to the other. But Burns couldn't see it; he had me written out altogether."

The majority of the stars Rolfe worked with "treated me very nicely." But there were exceptions: "Greta Garbo was very distant on *Ninotchka*. She was all business on the set; we rehearsed without her, then she came in and we shot the scene. John Barrymore was nice, but when he would drink he was extremely nasty with people... Barrymore was the kind of a guy who would take his pecker out of his pants and show it to you."

Over the course of his career, Sedan made one mistake that he regretted to the end. For want of an agent in the mid-1930s, he felt his best opportunities passed him by. "Director Leo McCarey wanted to put me under personal contract," he recalled. "I didn't have anybody to talk for me, and I didn't want to get under contract to a guy for $150 a week. I should've taken it, but I had nobody to advise me.

"I wanted to be in films what I was in the theater. People like Harold Stone, who played with me on Broadway, got somewhere in films because they had representation. I couldn't get an agent at that time; I should've stayed in New York and had an agent bring me out.

"I wouldn't advise young people to go into the entertainment field. They should have something else they can turn to until the opportunity presents itself. Unless they're absolutely dedicated and prepared for the hard knocks, they shouldn't go into it," he warned. "It's a cruel business."

While Sedan saw his face plastered on billboards in the 1960s — as a mustachioed saloon entertainer in a series of Pabst Blue Ribbon beer advertisements — he found acting jobs increasingly hard to come by as he got older. "If I had it to do again, I wouldn't be an actor — I'd be

Guest of honor at a 1980 convention.

a producer," he said late in life. "I'd be on the other end of the stick."

Long accustomed to the size of roles offered, he grew dispirited over the sheer lack of work available to performers of his vintage. Among the few film parts he won toward the end of his career where that of a German ambassador in *The Hindenburg*, a train conductor in *The World's Greatest Lover* and a rabbi in *The Frisco Kid*.

Rolfe, an aficionado of Oriental art who took up painting as a hobby, remained in reasonably good health until the year before his death. Plagued by recurring heart trouble, the 86-year-old actor collapsed and died of a coronary on September 16, 1982, in Pacific Palisades near West Los Angeles. He was survived by Beulah Sedan, his wife of 58 years, who has since passed away.

THE FILMS OF ROLFE SEDAN

No attempt has been made to list the films Sedan appeared in as an extra, circa 1908. Titles are unavailable for most of the shorts and features he made while under contract to Universal from 1921-1925. Film clips of the actor were used in two compilations, THE GOLDEN AGE OF COMEDY (1957) and LAUREL AND HARDY'S LAUGHING '20s (1965). The following list is representative but far from complete.

Shorts

THE LEATHER PUSHERS — Universal 1922
EVERY MAN FOR HIMSELF — Roach-Pathé 1924
IS MARRIAGE THE BUNK? — Roach-Pathé 1925
LOOKING FOR SALLY — Roach-Pathé 1925
MIGHTY LIKE A MOOSE — Roach-Pathé 1926
BROMO AND JULIET — Roach-Pathé 1926
BABY CLOTHES — Roach-Pathé 1926
YOU'RE DARN TOOTIN' — Roach-MGM 1928
DOUBLE WHOOPEE — Roach-MGM 1929
DAD'S DAY — Roach-MGM 1929
MEN O'WAR — Roach-MGM 1929 *scenes deleted*
ARABIAN TIGHTS — Roach-MGM 1933
LUNCHEON AT TWELVE — Roach-MGM 1933
MUSH AND MILK — Roach-MGM 1933
SNEAK EASILY — Roach-MGM 1933
DONE IN OIL — Roach-MGM 1934
ARBOR DAY — Roach-MGM 1936
HEADLINER NO. 1 — RKO Radio 1938
CHAMPAGNE FOR TWO — Paramount 1947

Features

MERRY-GO-ROUND — Universal 1923
THE HUNCHBACK OF NOTRE DAME — Universal 1923
SPORTING YOUTH — Universal 1924
EXCITEMENT — Universal 1924
THE DANGEROUS BLONDE — Universal 1924
LOVE AND GLORY — Universal 1924
YOUNG IDEAS — Universal 1924
THE MAD WHIRL — Universal 1924
THE PHANTOM OF THE OPERA — Universal 1925
SMOULDERING FIRES — Universal 1925
THE MERRY WIDOW — MGM 1925
MY OLD DUTCH — Universal 1926
BEAU GESTE — Paramount 1926
FIFTH AVENUE — Producers Distributing Corporation 1926

MAN TRAP — Paramount 1926
THE MAGIC FLAME — United Artists 1927
COMPASSION — Adamson 1927
THE DENVER DUDE — Universal 1927
UNCLE TOM'S CABIN — Universal 1927
SEVENTH HEAVEN — Fox 1927
SHOW PEOPLE — MGM 1928
THE ADORABLE CHEAT — Chesterfield 1928
REILLY OF RAINBOW DIVISION (Riley of the Rainbow Division) —
    Anchor 1928
CHINATOWN CHARLIE — First National 1928
CELEBRITY — Pathé 1928
MAN MADE WOMEN — Pathé 1928
LOVE AND THE DEVIL (The Comedy of Life) — First National 1929
THE IRON MASK — United Artists 1929
MAKING THE GRADE — Fox 1929
ONE HYSTERICAL NIGHT (No, No Napoleon) — Universal 1929
THE DANCE OF LIFE — Paramount 1929
STREET GIRL — RKO Radio 1929
SHOW GIRL IN HOLLYWOOD — First National 1930
MONTE CARLO — Paramount 1930
SWEETHEARTS AND WIVES — First National 1930
SWING HIGH — Pathé 1930
WHAT A WIDOW! — United Artists 1930
SWEET KITTY BELLAIRS — Warner Bros. 1930
CHILDREN OF PLEASURE — MGM 1930
PARAMOUNT ON PARADE — Paramount 1930
PARTY GIRL — Tiffany 1930
A LADY'S MORALS (The Soul Kiss) — MGM 1930
FINN AND HATTIE — Paramount 1931
JUST A GIGOLO (Dancing Partner) — MGM 1931
THE GALLOPING GHOST — Mascot 1931 [serial]
FIFTY MILLION FRENCHMEN — Warner Bros. 1931
MONKEY BUSINESS — Paramount 1931
THE WOMAN BETWEEN — RKO Radio 1931
THE DEVIL ON DECK — Sono Art-World Wide 1932
TROUBLE IN PARADISE — Paramount 1932
LOVE ME TONIGHT — Paramount 1932
EVENINGS FOR SALE — Paramount 1932
GRAND HOTEL — MGM 1932
70,000 WITNESSES — Paramount 1932
BACK STREET — Universal 1932
THE PASSIONATE PLUMBER — MGM 1932
WINNER TAKE ALL — Warner Bros. 1932
TEMPTATION'S WORKSHOP (Youth's Highway) — Mayfair 1932
THE MATCH KING — First National 1932
WHEN STRANGERS MARRY — Columbia 1933
COCKTAIL HOUR — Columbia 1933

Sedan (left), with William Austin (seated) and Roland Young in *Topper Takes a Trip* (1938).

DEVIL'S MATE — Monogram 1933
THE SIN OF NORA MORAN — Majestic 1933
THE WORLD GONE MAD — Majestic 1933
WHAT! NO BEER? — MGM 1933
DESIGN FOR LIVING — Paramount 1933
42ND STREET — Warner Bros. 1933
PRIVATE DETECTIVE 62 (Man Killer) — Warner Bros. 1933
TOPAZE — RKO Radio 1933
ADORABLE — Fox 1933
LAUGHING AT LIFE — Mascot 1933
THE DEVIL'S BROTHER (Fra Diavolo) — Roach-MGM 1933
REUNION IN VIENNA — MGM 1933
THE LITTLE GIANT — First National 1933
THE WORST WOMAN IN PARIS? — Fox 1933
THE WAY TO LOVE — Paramount 1933
SHE HAD TO SAY YES — First National 1933
WONDER BAR — First National 1934
LADIES SHOULD LISTEN — Paramount 1934
EVELYN PRENTICE — MGM 1934 *scenes deleted*
THE MERRY WIDOW — MGM 1934
LA VEUVE JOYEUSE — MGM 1934 [French version of
    THE MERRY WIDOW]
THE THIN MAN — MGM 1934
PALOOKA (Joe Palooka) — Reliance-UA 1934
THE MAN WHO RECLAIMED HIS HEAD — Universal 1934
KANSAS CITY PRINCESS — Warner Bros. 1934
NOW AND FOREVER — Paramount 1934
PARIS INTERLUDE (All Good Americans) — MGM 1934
A TALE OF TWO CITIES — MGM 1935
BROADWAY GONDOLIER — Warner Bros. 1935
CORONADO — Paramount 1935 *scenes deleted*
BROADWAY MELODY OF 1936 — MGM 1935
CHARLIE CHAN IN PARIS — Fox 1935

RUGGLES OF RED GAP — Paramount 1935
ALL THE KING'S HORSES (Be Careful, Young Lady) — Paramount 1935
$1,000 A MINUTE — Republic 1935
PARIS IN SPRING — Paramount 1935
A NIGHT AT THE OPERA — MGM 1935
MAD LOVE — MGM 1935
HERE COMES THE BAND — MGM 1935
LOTTERY LOVER — Fox 1935
SHIP CAFE (The Bouncer) — Paramount 1935
CORONADO — Paramount 1935
ROSE MARIE — MGM 1936
SMARTEST GIRL IN TOWN — RKO Radio 1936
ANYTHING GOES (Tops Is the Limit) — Paramount 1936
THE ACCUSING FINGER — Paramount 1936
UNDER TWO FLAGS — 20th Century-Fox 1936
THE SINGING MARINE — Warner Bros. 1937
SHALL WE DANCE — RKO Radio 1937
HIGH, WIDE AND HANDSOME — Paramount 1937
RHYTHM IN THE CLOUDS — Republic 1937
HITTING A NEW HIGH — RKO Radio 1937
100 MEN AND A GIRL — Universal 1937
THE FIREFLY — MGM 1937
DOUBLE OR NOTHING — Paramount 1937
THE GIRL SAID NO — Grand National 1937
CAFE METROPOLE — 20th Century-Fox 1937
FIGHT FOR YOUR LADY — RK0 1937
SOULS AT SEA — Paramount 1937
A TRIP TO PARIS — 20th Century-Fox 1938
LETTER OF INTRODUCTION — Universal 1938
STRANGE FACES — Universal 1938
THAT CERTAIN AGE — Universal 1938
PARADISE FOR THREE — MGM 1938
HOLIDAY — Columbia 1938
TOPPER TAKES A TRIP — Roach-UA 1938
ADVENTURE IN SAHARA — Columbia 1938
STOLEN HEAVEN — Paramount 1938
I'LL GIVE A MILLION — 20th Century-Fox 1938
BLUEBEARD'S EIGHTH WIFE — Paramount 1938
A DESPERATE ADVENTURE — Republic 1938
UNDER THE BIG TOP — Monogram 1938
THE STORY OF VERNON AND IRENE CASTLE — RKO Radio 1939
NINOTCHKA — MGM 1939
THE WIZARD OF OZ — MGM 1939
EVERYTHING HAPPENS AT NIGHT — 20th Century-Fox 1939
JUAREZ AND MAXIMILIAN — Torres 1939
THE MA N IN THE IRON MASK — United Artists 1939
SHE MARRIED A COP (Laughing Irish Hearts) — Republic 1939
CHARLIE CHAN IN CITY OF DARKNESS — 20th Century-Fox 1939

FLORIAN — MGM 1940
GOLDEN GLOVES — Paramount 1940
PRIVATE AFFAIRS — Universal 1940
I WAS AN ADVENTURESS — 20th Century-Fox 1940
LAUGHING AT DANGER — Monogram 1940
HUDSON'S BAY — 20th Century-Fox 1940
CHARLEY'S AUNT — 20th Century-Fox 1941
LAW OF THE TROPICS — Warner Bros. 1941
SAN ANTONIO ROSE — Universal 1941
ANGELS WITH BROKEN WINGS — Republic 1941
THAT UNCERTAIN FEELING — United Artists 1941
THE HORN BLOWS AT MIDNIGHT — Warner Bros. 1945
PEOPLE'S CHOICE — Planet 1946
THAT FORSYTE WOMAN — MGM 1949
NOT WANTED — Film Classics 1949
LET'S DANCE — Paramount 1950
MY FAVORITE SPY — Paramount 1951
A MILLIONAIRE FOR CHRISTY (The Golden Goose) —
    20th Century Fox 1951
SOMETHING TO LIVE FOR — Paramount 1952
APRIL IN PARIS — Warner Bros. 1952
GENTLEMEN PREFER BLONDES — 20th Century-Fox 1953
THE MISSISSIPPI GAMBLER — Universal 1953
SO THIS IS PARIS (Three Gobs in Paris) — Universal 1954
PHANTOM OF THE RUE MORGUE — Warner Bros. 1954
THE BIRDS AND THE BEES — Paramount 1956
SILK STOCKINGS — MGM 1957
BEDTIME STORY (King of the Mountain) — Universal 1964
McHALE'S NAVY — Universal 1964
36 HOURS — MGM 1964
THE ART OF LOVE — Universal 1965
HOW I SPENT MY SUMMER VACATION — Universal-NBC 1967
    [TV movie]
WAKE ME WHEN THE WAR IS OVER — Thomas-Spelling-ABC 1969
    [TV movie]
DARLING LILI — Paramount 1970
THE OUTSIDE MAN — United Artists 1973
CHINATOWN — Paramount 1974
YOUNG FRANKENSTEIN — 20th Century-Fox 1975
THE HINDENBURG — Universal 1975
THE HAPPY HOOKER GOES TO WASHINGTON —
    Cannon Releasing 1977
THE WORLD'S GREATEST LOVER — 20th Century-Fox 1977
LOVE AT FIRST BITE — American-International 1979 *scenes deleted*
THE FRISCO KID — Warner Bros. 1979
BEGGARMAN, THIEF — Universal-NBC 1979 [TV movie]
THE UNSEEN — World Northal 1981

Burt Mustin

Seventeen years ago, Burt Mustin sent a three-page handwritten letter, in answer to a fan's inquiry: "It is always a pleasure to hear from somebody who goes to the trouble of learning the name of that 'him again' character..." he observed. I was the recipient of that letter, which began a friendship that lasted until his death. It was always a pleasure to be in the company of that modest, amiable man, and I cherish the memory.

He imparted words of wisdom to Beaver Cleaver, matched wits with Clem Kadiddlehopper and outsmarted Sergeant Friday. He counseled Archie Bunker on growing old and shacked up with Mother Dexter. His face is familiar to anyone who has ever turned on a television set.

Burt Mustin got a kick out of being paid for something he did for nothing most of his life; he was 67 when his hobby became his profession. When he died early in 1977 he was one of the oldest actors in Hollywood — 92 years young — and one of the busiest: in 25 years, he had piled up over 370 TV appearances and roughly 70 feature films to his credit.

His characters glowed with the warmth of his own personality and crackled with his wit. The older he got the more in demand he was, and the more prominent his roles became. His wise-cracking delivery boys, slow thinking night watchmen and worldly bachelors never failed to get a laugh; in later years his lively song-and-dance routines on *All in the Family* and near-prehistoric jokes on *The Tonight Show* earned him celebrity status.

Burton H. Mustin was born in Pittsburgh February 8, 1884, to a venerable Philadelphia family. He liked to say he "turned pro" at the age of 6, when a drunk heard him singing on his way home from kindergarten and took him into the neighborhood saloon to sing for the crowd. "I went home after dark with my pockets full of money and got a licking for it," he recalled.

In 1903 he graduated from Pennsylvania Military College — where he was goalie on the class hockey team — with a degree in engineering. His plans to join his father's brokerage office were wiped out, along with the firm, by the Panic of '03. When he realized he

167

Mustin (seated) and college hockey teammates circa 1902.

"couldn't tell one end of a blueprint from the other," he ended up selling automobiles.

Before Mustin created a niche for himself in the role of the wise, witty and agile senior citizen, "I gave it away free for 50 years, acting and singing and dancing anywhere and everywhere. I was a member of the Savoyards, an all-male chorus that sang in the chorus of Gilbert and Sullivan operettas," he stated. "I sang in the church choir and in a barbershop quartet, and even did boffo roles with the Pittsburgh Opera."

When H.R. Burnside of the New York Hippodrome visited to direct one production, "I learned more in five weeks working with him than the rest of the time I was there," said Mustin. When he asked what his prospects were in show business, Burnside said he'd do just fine. But he told the novice, "You've got a home, a good job and you're having lots of fun — why leave?" The young amateur took the advice and stayed in his home town.

In 1921 Burt sang on the first weekly variety show ever broadcast, on pioneer station KDKA in Pittsburgh. "I was billed as the World's Worst Announcer," he mused. "We called ourselves the Air Cooled Gang because we plugged Franklin Air Cooled Cars, which I was selling at the time."

When auto manufacturers switched to the production of war materials at the outset of World War II — and there were no cars to sell — Mustin more or less retired, although he worked a variety of jobs. He continued to act and sing as a hobby when he and his wife moved to Tucson.

A combination of luck and talent resulted in Mustin's first paid acting job in 1950. When a movie producer arrived in Tucson and put out a call for anybody who could ride a horse, the former auto salesman won the role of the town marshal — a week's work — in *The Last Outpost* with Ronald Reagan.

Burt went to Phoenix the following year to play a janitor in an amateur production of *Detective Story*, which was being readied as a film. "William Wyler came over to see his star, Kirk Douglas, do the stage role. He liked what I did well enough to take me back to play the same part in the picture," recalled Mustin. "So I had an agent and a contract before I ever hit Hollywood — a nice way to break in."

Doovid Barskin, who became and remained Mustin's agent for 25 years, remembers, "I drove to Phoenix to see the play, to see some other people. Everybody told me how great Burt was; I said, 'Come to town. I'll represent you.' The Barskin Agency represented him from the day he arrived in Hollywood until the day he died. He was a wonderful character; there was no one like him."

With the enthusiastic support of his wife ("that girl of mine") and the aid of Barskin, the tall, lean actor with the bald pate soon found his talents much in demand. In *The Lusty Men* he chased Robert Mitchum out from under his house with a shotgun. In *A Lion Is in the Streets* he played the town's eldest eligible bachelor; in *Cattle Queen of Montana* he was a crotchety old doctor digging bullets out of a gunslinger.

He readily created an army of characters to people the backdrop of movies: a miner in *The Sheepman*, a butler in *The Thrill of It All*, a bailiff in *Son of Flubber*, a janitor in *Speedway* (in which he danced with his broom), a convict in *Dead Heat On A Merry-Go Round*, a liveryman in *Skin Game* and crusty Uncle Jeff in the musical, *Mame*.

While he supported some of Hollywood's biggest stars — and found most of them a pleasure to work with — Mustin regretted he never had the chance to perform alongside the likes of Spencer Tracy or Gary Cooper: "I would've been happy to carry a spear for any of those guys," he observed.

With Charles Fredericks (left), Jessica Tandy and Richard Beymer in
Hemingway's Adventures of a Young Man (1962).

Mustin was a favorite of TV producers from the beginning. During
the 1950s, '60s and '70s he appeared on nearly every show on the
air — or so it seemed. He guarded the underground vault on *The Jack
Benny Show*, sang barbershop quartet on *The Andy Griffith Show*
and was doctored on *Marcus Welby, M.D.* He turned up on *Gunsmoke* as a 104-year-old horsethief.

One of his more memorable parts was the recurring role of Gus,
the avuncular fireman who dispensed homespun philosophy and advice to Jerry Mathers on *Leave It To Beaver*. "I always try to relate a
character to my own experience," said Mustin. "I thought back to my
youth, and I remembered an old riverboat captain I knew, back in the
1890s. I based the character of Gus on him."

Jack Webb ("a hard taskmaster") hired Mustin as often as possible,
and gave him some of his best roles on the tube. Burt played an absent-
minded cat burglar on *Dragnet*, and returned on a later show as a
former detective who outwitted Webb. The actor also had four run-ins
with the police on Webb's *Adam 12*, in four different roles — notably

With Arthur Hunnicut and Guy Wilkinson (foreground) in a scene cut from
Cat Ballou (1965).

as a drunk who disrobed in a bar to display his physique. "I
don't think I'll get any more calls to appear nude for a while," he
cracked afterwards.

His favorite film role was that of a retired outlaw in *Cat Ballou*. In a
scene cut before release, Burt accused an opponent of cheating at
cards and drew a gun on him; he then pulled the trigger but found he
was out of ammunition.

In the follow-up — which remained in the film — he walked up to Kid
Shelleen (Lee Marvin) and asked, "Can loan me a bullet, Kid? You remember me, old…old…," he stammered, unable to remember his name.
"If you want to see one line stop a show, just watch yourself in this
one," director Elliot Silverstein told him in a letter. "The timing is
perfect."

While he won some meaty roles, particularly on TV, Mustin was
just as happy to do a walk-on or a one-line bit. The residuals often
compensated him for the size of the role: "If you can make one of
those little nuthin' parts stand out," he observed , "it really piles up."

As Mr. Quigley, with Jean Stapleton on CBS' *All in the Family* (1973).

With Queenie Smith on NBC's *The Funny Side*.

Mustin was no stranger to the cutting room floor, but he was especially irked when his guest appearance as "the world's oldest champion basketball player" was snipped from a Harlem Globetrotters' TV special. "They brought me out in a wheelchair and stood me up. I shot a basket, then they sat me back down and wheeled me off the court," he reported. "It was a *funny* bit."

Burt was hired on short notice for a role in *Dirty Dingus Magee*. No one talked to his agent or inquired about his horsemanship; upon arrival in Tucson, he found he was cast as an Indian Cavalry scout. "I told the producer, 'That ought to be interesting. There's just two things — I'm 85 and I don't ride.' One fall and I'd be all finished, at my age," said the actor, who was on the next plane home. "I had a little trouble, but I finally got paid for that one."

In 1971 Mustin found himself "locked up at NBC" for two weeks, taping a pilot for a weekly variety show called *The Funny Side* — in which he sang, danced and did calisthenics. "They nearly *ruined* an 87-year-old actor on that one," he noted. Burt co-starred with Gene

With Judith Lowry and Cloris Leachman on CBS' *Phyllis* (1976).

Kelly in the series that resulted that fall, but the show was canceled after 13 weeks.

His appearances on the popular *All In The Family* in 1973 earned him more publicity and recognition than he had ever received. As Mr. Quigley, a pajama-clad stranger found wandering the street, he was taken to the Bunker home and adopted as the family's grandfather. He returned on a later show to help Archie celebrate a birthday, and livened up the party with an energetic song and dance.

Toward the end of his career, Burt became Johnny Carson's favorite closing act on *The Tonight Show*, offering songs from the turn of the century and jokes that were older than he was. Carson often ran out of time before the nonagenarian could appear, but Mustin was unperturbed. "The money's not bad," he once commented, "considering I get three pay checks for one show."

Between roles he often engaged in a game of cards at the Hollywood Masquers Club with his close friend, veteran character actor Percy Helton, and other pals. A longtime member of SPEBSQSA (Society for the Preservation and Encouragement of Barbershop Quartet Singing in America), Mustin eagerly traveled around the country to participate in competitions.

"Hollywood is the only place in the world where you can work four

"The best 'they-went-thataway' actor in town."

days out of the month and loaf 26 and still make a good living," he often asserted. "The only trouble is to get the four." Mustin had less trouble finding "the four" than any other actor in his age bracket — especially as he got older.

Mustin, who drove a car until he was 90, remained in relatively good health until his last years. He was weak and frail when he taped a two-part episode of *Phyllis* in the fall of 1976, in which he married the tart-tongued Mother Dexter (Judith Lowry). But the show had been written for him and he was determined to fulfill his commitment to the producers — "the end of my blazing career," he joked — though he could hardly walk.

Burt was hospitalized the week after the taping, at the retirement home where he lived in Glendale. Lowry, 86, died that November, before the show was broadcast; Mustin himself was too ill to watch the program when it aired. When he died on January 28, 1977, the week before his 93rd birthday, a barbershop quartet sang at his funeral — Burt's last request.

Mustin was happy with his "little nuthin' parts" and always made the most of them; the less he had to work with, the more he did with it. "I'm the best 'they-went-thataway' actor in town," he often said, mockingly.

THE FILMS OF BURT MUSTIN

Mustin did not appear in BUS STOP (1956), as recorded elsewhere; he was slated for but did not appear in DIRTY DINGUS MAGEE (1970). Based on a list compiled by Mustin, and other sources.

THE LAST OUTPOST — Paramount 1951
DETECTIVE STORY — Paramount 1951
THE SELLOUT (County Line) — MGM 1952
WE'RE NOT MARRIED — 20th Century-Fox 1952 *scenes deleted*
JUST ACROSS THE STREET — Universal 1952
THE LUSTY MEN — RKO Radio 1952
TALK ABOUT A STRANGER — MGM 1952
THE SILVER WHIP — 20th Century-Fox 1953
ONE GIRL'S CONFESSION — Columbia 1953
A LION IS IN THE STREETS — Warner Bros. 1953
VICKI — 20th Century-Fox 1953
THE MOONLIGHTER — Warner Bros. 1953
HALF A HERO — MGM 1953
WITNESS TO MURDER — United Artists 1954
GYPSY COLT — MGM 1954
SHE COULDN'T SAY NO (She Had to Say Yes) — RKO Radio 1954
DAY OF TRIUMPH — Century Films 1954
EXECUTIVE SUITE — MGM 1954 *scenes deleted*
RIVER OF NO RETURN — 20th Century-Fox 1954 *scenes deleted*
CATTLE QUEEN OF MONTANA — RKO Radio·1954
SILVER LODE (Four Desperate Men) — RKO Radio 1954
THE DESPERATE HOURS — Paramount 1955
PRINCE OF PLAYERS — 20th Century-Fox 1955 *scenes deleted*
THE KENTUCKIAN — United Artists 1955
MAN WITH THE GUN — United Artists 1955
THE RETURN OF JACK SLADE — Allied Artists 1955
GREAT DAY IN THE MORNING — RKO Radio 1956
EDGE OF HELL — Universal 1956
STORM CENTER — Columbia 1956
THESE WILDER YEARS — MGM 1956
RAINTREE COUNTY — MGM 1957
THE SHEEPMAN — MGM 1958
RALLY 'ROUND THE FLAG, BOYS! — 20th Century-Fox 1958
THE FBI STORY — Warner Bros. 1959
HOME FROM THE HILL — MGM 1960
THE ADVENTURES OF HUCKLEBERRY FINN — MGM 1960
SNOW WHITE AND THE THREE STOOGES — 20th Century-Fox 1961
ALL FALL DOWN — MGM 1962

HEMINGWAY'S ADVENTURES OF A YOUNG MAN —
    20th Century-Fox 1962
THE THRILL OF IT ALL — Universal 1963
SON OF FLUBBER — Disney-Buena Vista 1963
TWILIGHT OF HONOR — MGM 1963
THE MISADVENTURES OF MERLIN JONES — Disney-Buena Vista 1964
WHAT A WAY TO GO! — 20th Century-Fox 1964
SEX AND THE SINGLE GIRL — Warner Bros. 1964
THE KILLERS (Ernest Hemingway's The Killers) — Universal 1964
CAT BALLOU — Columbia 1965
THE CINCINNATI KID — MGM 1965
THE ADVENTURES OF BULLWHIP GRIFFIN — Disney-Buena Vista 1966
THE GHOST AND MR. CHICKEN — Universal 1966
DEAD HEAT ON A MERRY-GO-ROUND — Columbia 1966
THE RELUCTANT ASTRONAUT — Universal 1967
SPEEDWAY — MGM 1968
THE SHAKIEST GUN IN THE WEST — Universal 1968 *scenes deleted*
THE LOVE BUG — Disney-Buena Vista 1969
THE WITCHMAKER (The Berserk) — Excelsior 1969
THE GREAT BANK ROBBERY — Warner Bros.-Seven Arts 1969
    scenes deleted
THE OVER-THE-HILL GANG — Thomas-Spelling-ABC 1969 [TV movie]
HAIL, HERO! — National General 1969
TIGER BY THE TAIL — Commonwealth United-American
    International Pictures 1970
THE OVER THE HILL GANG RIDES AGAIN — Thomas-Spelling-ABC
    1970 [TV movie]
SKIN GAME — Warner Bros. 1971
O'HARA, UNITED STATES TREASURY: OPERATION COBRA —
    Mark VII-Universal-CBS 1971 [TV movie]
A TIME FOR DYING — Etoile Distribution 1971 [no U.S. theatrical release]
NOW YOU SEE HIM, NOW YOU DON'T — Disney-Buena Vista 1972
MIRACLE ON 34TH STREET — 20th Century-Fox-CBS 1973 [TV movie]
MAME — Warner Bros. 1974
HERBIE RIDES AGAIN — Disney-Buena Vista 1974
BIG ROSE — CBS 1974 [TV movie]
MOBILE TWO — ABC 1975 [TV movie]
THE STRONGEST MAN IN THE WORLD — Disney-Buena Vista 1975
TRAIN RIDE TO HOLLYWOOD — Billy Jack Enterprises 1976
ARTHUR HAILEY'S THE MONEYCHANGERS — Paramount-NBC 1976
    [TV movie]
BAKER'S HAWK — Doty-Dayton Productions 1977

George Chandler

George Chandler had little enthusiasm for interviews in his later years. But he was wonderfully cooperative in spite of himself, and his power of recall was remarkable. He chose his anecdotes carefully at first — he wanted to save it for the book he was writing — but eventually he opened up. And I was all ears, as the story of his career began to unfold.

Early in his career the late George Chandler won respect as a hardworking, easy-going fellow. His sterling reputation — and a knack for playing abrasive wise guys and gullible dupes — made him one of the most prolific actors in Hollywood. From his debut in a 1927 Jack Duffy comedy, to his swan song in a 1979 episode of *Lou Grant*, Chandler stepped before the cameras over 700 times.

Chandler's willingness to perform for the most demanding directors in town and do what he was told proved the key to his survival in the film business. "You don't have to get tough if you're diplomatic," asserted the actor, who was perhaps best known for his characterization of Uncle Petrie on the popular *Lassie* TV series.

Fritz Lang, who directed him in *Fury* and *The Return of Frank James*, was "pretty rough with some of his actors," Chandler recalled, toward the end of his long career. "I wouldn't take any guff from him, and he respected me. I took nothing, but I was polite about it. Fritz was so wound up getting a good scene and a good picture he'd forget to be a gentleman — and I would remind him.

"Lang was such a perfectionist, he didn't care how he did things. He made life miserable for actors. But Spencer Tracy and Walter Brennan — boy, they put the thumb down on him so fast he became a pussycat; he had quite a time with those two guys."

A native of Waukegan, Illinois, George Chandler was born June 30, 1898 (not 1902, as generally recorded). He first decided an actor's life would suit him at the age of 12, when his eighth-grade class put on a scene from *A Midsummer Night's Dream*.

"None of the kids wanted to wear the donkey's head; they wanted their fathers and mothers and all their friends to recognize them. So the teacher points to me and says, 'You're going to play Bottom.' The night we did it," said Chandler, "I put the donkey head on and went out on stage. I got such a reception I couldn't believe it. When I finished the scene, the applause continued. I had to come back and take a bow. And I said, 'I'm going to be an actor. I love the applause.'"

Chandler, who took violin lessons as a child, made his entry into show business following a stint in World War I as a second lieutenant. "I answered an ad in the *Tribune*: 'Wanted — musicians who can sing for chautauqua act.' The act was called The Fighting Americans — we all wore our uniforms so we could get a little sympathy from the audience," he noted.

In 1919 he quit the Coit-Alber Chautauqua circuit to go into vaudeville as "George Chandler, the Musical Nut." (The sobriquet was well earned: at the finish, he held the fiddle over his head and did the Russian hockstep; he also played a musical saw.)

The energetic young entertainer — who paid his way through the University of Illinois playing the fiddle — did his act in night clubs as well. "They didn't call 'em that in Chicago," he observed. "They were cabarets, and most of them were run by gangsters. One of the clubs, the Silver Slipper, was owned by Ruth Etting's husband [Moe Snyder]. A guy came in to visit me one night. He said, 'If anybody ever gives you any trouble, just call me and I'll have 'em rubbed out.'"

Anxious to break into the movies, Chandler asked everybody, "Who do you know in pictures?" When a theater manager gave him a letter of introduction to Carl Laemmle at Universal, the aspiring actor took a train to California — only to find the letter wouldn't get him past the studio gate.

One night he was playing the local Fanchon-Marco circuit and decided to give a promising amateur some advice. The young man's sister happened to be a Universal contract player; a talent scout caught Chandler's act and he was on his way.

Chandler was making $200 a week in 1927 when he quit vaudeville to accept Laemmle's offer of $75. A starring role in a series of short subjects called "The Tenderfoot Thrillers" — and billing above the title — soon compensated him for the cut in pay. As a bonus, the publicist trimmed four years off his age.

The two-reel comedy westerns required a lot of acrobatics on Chandler's part, a la Buster Keaton; he even wore a pork pie hat to capitalize on the similarity. The budding comic then moved to Educational Pictures, where he was directed by William Goodrich — alias Keaton's mentor, Roscoe "Fatty" Arbuckle. A series of Edgar Kennedy two-reelers followed.

Typical of Chandler's earliest feature roles was *The Kid's Clever*, starring Glenn Tryon. ("I took a 40-foot fall off the deck of a ship," he recalled. "I was loaded at the time.") He found himself much in demand after playing Marion Davies' boy friend in *The Floradora Girl*

Chandler makes *A Clean Sweep* in this 1928 Tenderfoot Thriller.

With James Cagney in *Picture Snatcher* (1933).

(1930), thanks in part to the attendant newspaper publicity — courtesy of Davies' real-life paramour, William Randolph Hearst.

The actor essayed almost every conceivable role in the years that followed. In *Footlight Parade* he was a drugstore clerk who sold aspirin to James Cagney; in *It's in the Bag*, he was an elevator operator who tried to resolve a lover's quarrel. In *Arizona*, opposite William Holden, he played against type as a villain; in *Dead Reckoning*, he was the valet who served Humphrey Bogart a drugged drink.

Regardless of the part — or the size of it — he proved ready, willing and able; as a result, he worked constantly, often without billing. He was seen as a photographer in *Nothing Sacred*, a chauffeur in the *Shadow* series opposite Kane Richmond, a typesetter in *Jesse James*, a soldier in *The Story of G.I. Joe*, a telegraph operator in *The Miracle of the Bells* and a motorcycle cop in *The Next Voice You Hear*.

"I was a bit player," he said, "and I admit it. But I would sometimes do two pictures a day. I'd be on one, my agent would call and say, 'What time you gonna get through?' I'd say, 'I'm through now.' He'd say, 'Hop over to MGM, they got a bit for you there.' I was pretty

With Humphrey Bogart in *Dead Reckoning* (1947).

busy." He was often cast as a newspaper reporter: "Frank McHugh and myself had arguments — who played more reporters, he or I. I played 'em for years; I started dying my hair when it got a little gray so I could still play 'em "

When William Wellman was having trouble on *A Star is Born* (1937), his assistant recommended Chandler for the role of a messenger boy. "Bill had already had two actors play this part and he didn't like either of them. We did the scene in one take, and he said, 'You're wonderful. You'll be with me in my next picture.' I said, 'Well, thank you, Mr. Wellman, but I've heard that so many times I have to say, I think you're full of shit.' He said, 'You just wait, you sweet son of a bitch. You'll be with me.'"

Chandler (described in Wellman's autobiography as a friend "who would give me literally the shirt off his back") became the director's one-man stock company. He appeared in almost every picture Wellman made for the next two decades, including such memorable ones as *Beau Geste*, *Roxie Hart* (the actor's favorite, in which he played Ginger Rogers' obnoxious husband) and *The Ox-Bow Incident*.

Wellman was preparing to film Kipling's *The Light That Failed* when "I told him, 'There's one I can't be in, because I do the lousiest British accent.' He said, 'You wait, you sweet SOB, I'll show you.' In a week I get a script and the cast sheet has the name of a character, a reporter 'who has such a bad case of laryngitis he can't talk.' I didn't have to say a word.

"I was with Bill at the end; I loved the man and he reciprocated. He had fun, but he got the job done," asserted Chandler. "They called him 'Wild Bill' but he wasn't wild — just full of hell, that's all. He liked to laugh and he liked to have fun."

Another fun-loving co-worker was Carole Lombard, who showed up with a hangover the first day of shooting on *The Princess Comes Across* (1936). "She said, 'Pa [Clark Gable] and I really tied one on last night.' She got to her first speech and her eyes turned glassy; she was in a fog. Bill Howard, the director, said, 'We gotta shoot; the time's going.' She said to me, 'Look, I'm gone. But I remember the first speech. Will you do me a favor, Georgie? When I get the first speech off, will you blow the next one?' I said, 'Sure.'

"She did it fine, it came to my line and I blew it," said Chandler. "Howard yelled 'Cut.' He said, 'For Christ's sake, Carole was just great and you had to blow the whole thing.' He just ate me up and down. Carole says to Bill, 'I'm sure Georgie can get it right. Let's go.' She ripped through that scene in one take like the pro she was. When we got through, she said, 'Thank you, Georgie. That was all I needed.'"

Far more trying was the experience of playing W.C. Fields' way-ward son Chester in *The Fatal Glass of Beer*. "First day on the set," said Chandler, "Fields came in followed by a Filipino boy with a big tray of martinis. He said, 'Have a martini, George.' I said 'Bill, are you out of your mind? It's 8 o'clock in the morning.' He said, 'You'll be sorry.'"

Later, in his big scene, Chandler was seated at the head of a table with the comedian on one side and Rosemary Theby (as Fields' wife) on the other. "Fields had nothing to do in this scene except look up every once in a while and say, 'Yes, Chester.' He got a bucket and hid it behind him and came back to his seat and put it down by his feet. I thought, 'What's he trying to do?'

"I had the dialog, pages of it. I start and all of a sudden I look at Bill and he pulls that pail out and he's got his foot stuck in it. I'm trying not to look at it; the crew members are falling off their seats. He was grunting and groaning, 'Yes, Chester,' trying to get his foot out of the bucket.

As Amos in *Roxie Hart* (1942) — his favorite role.

"Finally it was over and the director [Clyde Bruckman] said, 'Beautiful. Print it.' I said 'Are you crazy? Did you see what that dirty SOB was doing with that bucket? You can't print it.' He said, 'It's beautiful, we print it and that's it.' So I went up to Bill. I said, 'Look, I'll make a deal with you. I'll have a martini with you every morning on the promise that you won't screw up any more of my scenes.' I had to drink with him the whole week."

Chandler never saw the two-reel comedy until decades later, when he was invited to a W.C. Fields film festival. "I said, 'I wouldn't see it if you paid me.' My wife said, 'Oh, let's see it just for the fun of it.'" The screening was a revelation: "I'd been framed," he contended, "and they were all in on it. They told me it was a three-shot. You know what it was? A tight close-up of me! You never saw Bill, you never saw the bucket or heard it. When the film was over I said, 'You know, I've hated that guy for 45 years. When I get to heaven I'm going to go up and apologize.'"

The actor had played hundreds of parts by the time he was cast as kindly old Uncle Petrie Martin in the long-running *Lassie* series, in 1957. While the show brought him greater recognition than he had ever had, he left after two seasons because "I got tired of playing second fiddle to a dog."

Chandler won perhaps the most important role of his career in 1960, when he succeeded Ronald Reagan as president of the Screen Actor's Guild. A staunch supporter of SAG since its inception in 1933, he had been on the board of directors for 14 years, and served as treasurer for nearly as long.

"The Guild changed the whole picture," he maintained. "Before they came in there was a blacklist, and if you didn't do what the studio asked you to do they put you the list. I would work all night and all day and only get my regular salary; we'd work Saturdays and up until daybreak Sundays with no overtime, no protection of any kind."

When Chandler and Reagan were negotiating with producers for TV residuals, in addition to pension and welfare, they took the "diplomatic" approach. By agreeing to give up rerun money for 1948-60 productions, they were given residuals from 1960 on and $300,000 to start SAG's pension and welfare fund.

"I don't know how many actors said, 'You sold us down the river, giving up that post '48 residual.' I told them, 'You've got it from '60 on and that's were the money will be made. The day will come when you'll have to retire from this business and you'll come on your knees and thank the Guild for getting you a pension and welfare plan.' Now they thank me," said Chandler, who served as president through 1963.

As Uncle Petrie, with Jon Provost in CBS' *Lassie*.

Concurrent with his starring role in SAG, Chandler played Ichabod Adams in the short-lived TV series *Ichabod and Me*. During his last term in office, he lost his wife of 27 years, the former Catherine Ward; in 1968, he married Helen Gutcheon.

During the Vietnam War he served as Chairman of the Hollywood Overseas Committee, recruiting James Stewart, John Wayne and other stars to visit American troops. Chandler remained active in films and TV in his later years; he did a stint on the daytime soap opera *General Hospital* and appeared in such movies as *Every Which Way But Loose*, as the Department of Motor Vehicles clerk.

At a party marking his 80th birthday in 1978, the actor told guests, "You're all invited to my 90th — don't any of you stand me up." But his health began to deteriorate after a near-fatal bout with pneumonia the following year, and he developed Alzheimer's disease. Forced to retire, he continued to play golf, long his favorite recreation, and wrote his memoirs (*Your Face Looks Familiar*, as yet unpublished).

On June 10, 1985 — three weeks before his 87th birthday — Chandler died of complications following cancer surgery, at a hospital in Panorama City, California. He was survived by his second wife, three sons (from his first marriage) and six grandchildren.

The actor at his home in Sherman Oaks, California, in 1978.

THE FILMS OF GEORGE CHANDLER

Chandler appeared in numerous two-reel westerns and comedies at Universal, as well as Christie and Educational shorts, in addition to those listed below. He made roughly 75 shorts in all, and perhaps 400 features. Despite Chandler's contention that he was in every William Wellman film from 1937-1958, he does not appear in YELLOW SKY (1949), IT'S A BIG COUNTRY (1952), TRACK OF THE CAT (1954), BLOOD ALLEY (1955), DARBY'S RANGERS (1958) or LAFAYETTE ESCADRILLE (1958). Nor does he appear in STRANGE CONQUEST (1946), HAZARD (1948) or ONE MORE TIME (1971), as recorded elsewhere. Based on a list compiled by Chandler, and other sources.

Shorts

A FIGHTING TENDERFOOT — Universal 1928
SAPS AND SADDLES — Universal 1928
A DANGEROUS DUDE — Universal 1928
A CLEAN SWEEP — Universal 1928
A TENDERFOOT HERO — Universal 1928
TWO GUN MORGAN — Universal 1929
A RIDING ROMEO — Universal 1929
RED ROMANCE — Universal 1929
A THRILL HUNTER — Universal 1929
A CLOSE CALL — Universal 1929
A TENDERFOOT TERROR — Universal 1929
THE GO GET 'EM KID — Universal 1929
IT HAPPENED IN HOLLYWOOD — Universal 1930
PURE AND SIMPLE — RKO Radio 1930
COWSLIPS — RKO Radio 1931
THE BACK PAGE — Educational 1931
LURE OF HOLLYWOOD (Hollywood Girl) — Educational 1931
UP POPS THE DUKE — Educational 1931
THE WIDE OPEN SPACES — Masquers Club-RKO Radio 1931
THE BRIDE'S BEREAVEMENT OR THE SNAKE IN THE GRASS —
    Masquers Club-RKO Radio 1932
THE FATAL GLASS OF BEER — Sennett-Paramount 1933
SOAK THE POOR (Crime Does Not Pay) — MGM 1937
COMMUNITY FINANCE — Wilding 1944 [industrial]
MORGAN'S FOLLY — MGM 1945
DON'T BE A SUCKER — 20th Century-Fox 1946
SO YOU WANT TO BE IN PICTURES — Warner Bros. 1947
SWEET CHEAT — RKO Radio 1949
KNUCKLEHEAD — Standard Oil-Wilding 1949 [industrial]

Features

THE CLOUD DODGER — Universal 1928
THE KID'S CLEVER — Universal 1929
THE VIRGINIAN — Paramount 1929
BLACK HILLS — Big Three 1929
VAGABOND LOVER — RKO Radio 1929
THE WOMAN FROM HELL (Lady From Hell) — Fox 1929
THE FLORADORA GIRL — MGM 1930
THE LIGHT OF WESTERN STARS — Paramount 1930
IN GAY MADRID — MGM 1930
ONLY SAPS WORK — Paramount 1930
SOUP TO NUTS — Fox 1930
THE LAST DANCE — Audible Pictures 1930
LEATHERNECKING — RKO Radio 1930
A HOLY TERROR — Fox 1931
MAN OF THE WORLD (Gentleman of the Streets) — Paramount 1931
DOCTOR'S WIVES — Fox 1931
TOO MANY COOKS — RKO Radio 1931
THE WOMAN BETWEEN — RKO Radio 1931
EVERYTHING'S ROSIE — RKO Radio 1931
BLESSED EVENT — Warner Bros. 1932
ME AND MY GAL — Fox 1932
BEAST OF THE CITY — MGM 1932
WINNER TAKE ALL — Warner Bros. 1932
THE FAMOUS FERGUSON CASE — First National 1932
UNION DEPOT — First National 1932
THE STRANGE LOVE OF MOLLY LOUVAIN — First National 1932
THE TENDERFOOT — First National 1932
AFRAID TO TALK (Merry-Go-Round) — Universal 1932
IS MY FACE RED? — RKO Radio 1932
THE SPORT PARADE — RKO Radio 1932
BUREAU OF MISSING PERSONS — First National 1933
ELMER THE GREAT — First National 1933
FOOTLIGHT PARADE — Warner Bros. 1933
PICTURE SNATCHER — Warner Bros. 1933
THE WHITE SISTER — MGM 1933
LADY KILLER — Warner Bros. 1933
THE POWER AND THE GLORY — Fox 1933
CENTRAL AIRPORT (Hello, Central) — Warner Bros. 1933
SHE HAD TO SAY YES — First National 1933
THE LIFE OF JIMMY DOLAN — Warner Bros. 1933
SON OF A SAILOR — Warner Bros. 1933
THE KEYHOLE — Warner Bros. 1933
THE KENNEL MURDER CASE — Warner Bros. 1933
PARACHUTE JUMPER — Warner Bros. 1933
MUSIC IN THE AIR — Fox 1934

With W.C. Fields in *The Fatal Glass of Beer* (1933).

EVELYN PRENTICE — MGM 1934   *scenes deleted*
HI, NELLIE! — Warner Bros. 1934
DARK HAZARD — First National 1934
FOG OVER FRISCO — First National 1934
HE WAS HER MAN — Warner Bros. 1934
20 MILLION SWEETHEARTS (Hot Air, Rhythm in the Air) —
    Warner Bros. 1934
HAPPINESS AHEAD — Warner Bros. 1934
BIG HEARTED HERBERT — Warner Bros. 1934
SIX DAY BIKE RIDER — First National 1934
STAR OF MIDNIGHT — RKO Radio 1935
THE GILDED LILY — Paramount 1935
FRONT PAGE WOMAN — Warner Bros. 1935
THE MURDER MAN — MGM 1935
STARS OVER BROADWAY — Warner Bros. 1935
MARY BURNS, FUGITIVE — Paramount 1935
THE WOMAN IN RED — First National 1935
THE CASE OF THE LUCKY LEGS — First National 1935
WELCOME HOME — Fox 1935
WHILE THE PATIENT SLEPT — First National 1935
BROADWAY GONDOLIER — Warner Bros. 1935
SPRING TONIC (Man-Eating Tiger) — Fox 1935
OLD HUTCH — MGM 1936
GOD'S COUNTRY AND THE WOMAN — Warner Bros. 1936
FLYING HOSTESS — Universal 1936
ALL AMERICAN CHUMP (Chain Lightning) — MGM 1936
HIGH TENSION — 20th Century-Fox 1936
SING, BABY, SING — 20th Century-Fox 1936

THE ACCUSING FINGER — Paramount 1936
THE COUNTRY DOCTOR — 20th Century-Fox 1936
FURY — MGM 1936
LIBELED LADY — MGM 1936
THREE MEN ON A HORSE — First National 1936
PENNIES FROM HEAVEN — Columbia 1936
REUNION — 20th Century-Fox 1936
HERE COMES TROUBLE — 20th Century-Fox 1936
SWORN ENEMY — MGM 1936
THE PRINCESS COMES ACROSS — Paramount 1936
NEIGHBORHOOD HOUSE — Roach-MGM 1936
WOMEN ARE TROUBLE — MGM 1936
SPEED — MGM 1936
WOMAN CHASES MAN — Goldwyn-United Artists 1937
A STAR IS BORN — Selznick-United Artists 1937
NOTHING SACRED — Selznick-United Artists 1937
BIG TOWN GIRL — 20th Century-Fox 1937
CHARLIE CHAN AT THE OLYMPICS — 20th Century-Fox 1937
MAYTIME — MGM 1937
SMALL TOWN BOY — Grand National 1937
DANGER! LOVE AT WORK — 20th Century-Fox 1937
WAKE UP AND LIVE — 20th Century-Fox 1937
ONE MILE FROM HEAVEN — 20th Century-Fox 1937
SARATOGA — MGM 1937
NANCY STEELE IS MISSING — 20th Century-Fox 1937
THE SINGING MARINE — Warner Bros. 1937.
THEY GAVE HIM A GUN — MGM 1937
BEG, BORROW OR STEAL — MGM 1937
DANGEROUS NUMBER — MGM 1937
LOVE ON TOAST — Paramount 1937
TIME OUT FOR ROMANCE — 20th Century-Fox 1937
LIVE, LOVE AND LEARN — MGM 1937
RIDING ON AIR — RKO Radio 1937
WOMAN-WISE — 20th Century-Fox 1937
THE JONES FAMILY IN HOT WATER — 20th Century-Fox 1937
THE GO-GETTER — Warner Bros. 1937
FAIR WARNING — 20th Century-Fox 1937
A FAMILY AFFAIR — MGM 1937
BIG CITY — MGM 1937
UP THE RIVER — 20th Century-Fox 1938
ONE WILD NIGHT — 20th Century-Fox 1938
MAN-PROOF — MGM 1938
GATEWAY — 20th Century-Fox 1938
SECRETS OF A NURSE — Universal 1938
MEN WITH WINGS — Paramount 1938
HARD TO GET — Warner Bros. 1938
MAD MISS MANTON — RKO Radio 1938

IN OLD CHICAGO — 20th Century-Fox 1938
MANNEQUIN — MGM 1938
THE SHINING HOUR — MGM 1938
BLOCKHEADS — Roach-MGM 1938 *scenes deleted*
PROFESSOR BEWARE — Paramount 1938
THE COWBOY AND THE LADY — Goldwyn-United Artists 1938
CHECKERS — 20th Century-Fox 1938
SHOPWORN ANGEL — MGM 1938
THERE GOES MY HEART — Roach-United Artists 1938
MR. MOTO'S GAMBLE — 20th Century-Fox 1938
THREE LOVES HAS NANCY — MGM 1938
THE LAST EXPRESS — Universal 1938
BREAKING THE ICE — RKO Radio 1938
EVERYBODY'S BABY — 20th Century-Fox 1938
JOY OF LIVING — RKO Radio 1938
RASCALS (Little Gypsy) — 20th Century-Fox 1938
THREE COMRADES — MGM 1938
VALLEY OF THE GIANTS — Warner Bros. 1938
VIVACIOUS LADY — RKO Radio 1938
IT'S A WONDERFUL WORLD — MGM 1939
20,000 MEN A YEAR — 20th Century-Fox 1939
FAST AND FURIOUS — MGM 1939
EVERYTHING'S ON ICE — RKO Radio 1939
JESSE JAMES — 20th Century-Fox 1939
KING OF THE TURF — United Artists 1939
SECOND FIDDLE — 20th Century-Fox 1939
I STOLE A MILLION — Universal 1939
CALLING ALL MARINES — Republic 1939
BEAU GESTE — Paramount 1939
MR. SMITH GOES TO WASHINGTON — Columbia 1939
EXILE EXPRESS — Grand National 1939
THE FLYING IRISHMAN — RKO Radio 1939
THE LIGHT THAT FAILED — Paramount 1939
WHILE NEW YORK SLEEPS — 20th Century-Fox 1939
I'M FROM MISSOURI — Paramount 1939
MADE FOR EACH OTHER — Selznick-United Artists 1939
THE JONES FAMILY IN HOLLYWOOD — 20th Century-Fox 1939
MR. MOTO TAKES A VACATION — 20th Century-Fox 1939
BLONDIE MEETS THE BOSS — Columbia 1939
SECRET OF DR. KILDARE — MGM 1939
YOUNG MR. LINCOLN — 20th Century-Fox 1939
ST. LOUIS BLUES — Paramount 1939
BOY SLAVES — RKO Radio 1939
THOU SHALT NOT KILL — Republic 1939
MANHATTAN HEARTBEAT — 20th Century-Fox 1940
MELODY RANCH — Republic 1940
THE RETURN OF FRANK JAMES — 20th Century-Fox 1940

With Mantan Moreland (far left), Benson Fong and Sidney Toler in *The Shanghai Cobra* (1945).

BROADWAY MELODY OF 1940 — MGM 1940
ABE LINCOLN IN ILLINOIS — RKO Radio 1940
CHARTER PILOT — 20th Century-Fox 1940
DR. KILDARE GOES HOME — MGM 1940
EDISON THE MAN — MGM 1940
LITTLE OLD NEW YORK — 20th Century-Fox 1940
THE MAN WHO WOULDN'T TALK — 20th Century-Fox 1940
SHOOTING HIGH — 20th Century-Fox 1940
FORGOTTEN GIRLS — Republic 1940
TRAIL OF THE VIGILANTES — Universal 1940
ARIZONA — Columbia 1940
HELLZAPOPPIN' — Universal 1941
WESTERN UNION — 20th Century-Fox 1941
REACHING FOR THE SUN — Paramount 1941
THE GAY VAGABOND — Republic 1941
BUY ME THAT TOWN — Paramount 1941
BROADWAY LIMITED — Roach-United Artists 1941
TOBACCO ROAD — 20th Century-Fox 1941
DANCE HALL — 20th Century-Fox 1941
MODEL WIFE — Universal 1941
OBLIGING YOUNG LADY — RKO Radio 1941
PRIVATE NURSE — 20th Century-Fox 1941
REPENT AT LEISURE — RKO Radio 1941
THREE SONS O'GUNS — Warner Bros. 1941
SLEEPERS WEST — 20th Century-Fox 1941
THE MAD DOCTOR — Paramount 1941

MOUNTAIN MOONLIGHT — Republic 1941
DOUBLE DATE — Universal 1941
REMEMBER THE DAY — 20th Century-Fox 1941
A GIRL, A GUY AND A GOB — RKO Radio 1941
LOOK WHO'S LAUGHING — RKO Radio 1941 *scenes deleted*
MAN AT LARGE — 20th Century-Fox 1941
DESIGN FOR SCANDAL — MGM 1941
MOUNTAIN MOONLIGHT — Republic 1941
THAT OTHER WOMAN — 20th Century-Fox 1942
HERE WE GO AGAIN — RKO Radio 1942
HIGHWAYS BY NIGHT — RKO Radio 1942
THE GREAT GILDERSLEEVE — RKO Radio 1942
CALL OUT THE MARINES — RKO Radio 1942
ROXIE HART — 20th Century-Fox 1942
THE GREAT MAN'S LADY — Paramount 1942
FOREST RANGERS — Paramount 1942
ISLE OF MISSING MEN (Isle of Terror) — Monogram 1942
NIGHT IN NEW ORLEANS — Paramount 1942
SCATTERGOOD SURVIVES A MURDER (The Cat's Claw Murder Mystery)
    — RKO Radio 1942
SECRETS OF THE UNDERGROUND (The Corpse Came COD, Mr. District
    Attorney) — Republic 1942
PRIVATE BUCKAROO — Universal 1942
A TRAGEDY AT MIDNIGHT — Republic 1942
THUNDER BIRDS — 20th Century-Fox 1942
PARDON MY SARONG — Universal 1942
CASTLE IN THE DESERT — 20th Century-Fox 1942
ARE HUSBANDS NECESSARY? — Paramount 1942
THE POWERS GIRL — United Artists 1942
A SCREAM IN THE DARK (The Morgue Is Always Open) — Republic 1943
HERS TO HOLD — Universal 1943
LADY OF BURLESQUE (The G-String Murders) — United Artists 1943
JOHNNY COME LATELY — United Artists 1943
THE OX-BOW INCIDENT — 20th Century-Fox 1943
SWING FEVER — MGM 1943
LET'S FACE IT — Paramount 1943
SWEET ROSIE O'GRADY — 20th Century-Fox 1943
NEVER A DULL MOMENT — Universal 1943
THE GREAT GILDERSLEEVE — RKO Radio 1943
CITY WITHOUT MEN — Columbia 1943
SWING-SHIFT MAISIE — MGM 1943
THEY GOT ME COVERED — Goldwyn-RKO Radio 1943
HERE COMES ELMER — Republic 1943
MY KINGDOM FOR A COOK — Columbia 1943
A NIGHT TO REMEMBER — Columbia 1943
HI BUDDY — Universal 1943
TALL IN THE SADDLE — RKO Radio 1944

BUFFALO BILL — 20th Century-Fox 1944
IT HAPPENED TOMMORROW — United Artists 1944
SINCE YOU WENT AWAY — Selznick-United Artists 1944
GOIN' TO TOWN — RKO Radio 1944
IRISH EYES ARE SMILING — 20th Century-Fox 1944
WING AND A PRAYER — 20th Century-Fox 1944
THREE MEN IN WHITE — MGM 1944
STEP LIVELY — RKO Radio 1944
THE CHINESE CAT — Monogram 1944
ALLERGIC TO LOVE — Universal 1944
BRIDE BY MISTAKE — RKO Radio 1944
HI, BEAUTIFUL (Slick Chick) — Universal 1944
JOHNNY DOESN'T LIVE HERE ANY MORE (And So They Were Married)
    — Monogram 1944
THIS MAN'S NAVY — MGM 1945
STRANGE CONFESSION (The Missing Head) — Universal 1945
CAPTAIN EDDIE — 20th Century-Fox 1945
COLONEL EFFINGHAM'S RAID — 20th Century-Fox 1945
THE STORY OF G.I. JOE — United Artists 1945
IT'S IN THE BAG — United Artists 1945
LADY ON A TRAIN — Universal 1945
TELL IT TO A STAR — Republic 1945
MAN FROM OKLAHOMA — Republic 1945
WITHOUT LOVE — MGM 1945
PARDON MY PAST — Columbia 1945
INCENDIARY BLONDE — Paramount 1945
SEE MY LAWYER — Universal 1945
PATRICK THE GREAT — Universal 1945
THE SHANGHAI COBRA — Monogram 1945
THE SHADOW RETURNS — Monogram 1946
THE LAST CROOKED MILE — Republic 1946
LOVER COME BACK — Universal 1946
A GUY COULD CHANGE — Republic 1946
BEHIND THE MASK — Monogram 1946
BECAUSE OF HIM — Universal 1946
THE FRENCH KEY — Republic 1946
GLASS ALIBI — Republic 1946
HELDORADO — Republic 1946
SO GOES MY LOVE — Universal 1946
MASK OF DIJON — PRC 1946
LITTLE GIANT — Universal 1946
GALLANT JOURNEY — Columbia 1946
THE KID FROM BROOKLYN — Goldwyn-RKO Radio 1946
THE MISSING LADY — Monogram 1946
STRANGE IMPERSONATION — Republic 1946
SUSPENSE — Monogram 1946
RENDEZVOUS WITH ANNIE — Republic 1946

BLACK ANGEL — Universal 1946
MICHIGAN KID — Universal 1947
DEAD RECKONING — Columbia 1947
IT'S A JOKE, SON — PRC 1947
KILLER McCOY — MGM 1947
I'LL BE YOURS — Universal 1947
MAGIC TOWN — RKO Radio 1947
IT HAD TO BE YOU — Columbia 1947
SUDDENLY IT'S SPRING — Paramount 1947
NIGHTMARE ALLEY — 20th Century-Fox 1947
THE SECRET LIFE OF WALTER MITTY — Goldwyn-RKO Radio 1947
SADDLE PALS — Republic 1947
ROAD TO RIO — Paramount 1947
NIGHT SONG (Memory of Love, Counterpoint) — RKO Radio 1947
SINBAD THE SAILOR — RKO Radio 1947
THE VIGILANTES RETURN — Universal 1947
HOLLOW TRIUMPH (The Scar, The Man Who Murdered Himself) —
    Eagle Lion 1948
ALIAS A GENTLEMAN — MGM 1948
THE COBRA STRIKES — Eagle Lion 1948
THE GIRL FROM MANHATTAN — United Artists 1948
THE IRON CURTAIN — 20th Century-Fox 1948
THE MIRACLE OF THE BELLS — RKO Radio 1948
RACE STREET — RKO Radio 1948
SILVER RIVER — Warner Bros. 1948
THE PALEFACE — Paramount 1948
THE PIRATE — MGM 1948
SONS OF ADVENTURE — Republic 1948
THE HUNTED — Monogram 1948
LIGHTNIN' IN THE FOREST — Republic 1948
YOU WERE MEANT FOR ME — 20th Century-Fox 1948
HOMICIDE (Night Beat) — Warner Bros. 1949
ONCE MORE, MY DARLING — Universal-International 1949
CANADIAN PACIFIC — 20th Century-Fox 1949
THE HOUSE ACROSS THE STREET — Warner Bros. 1949
KNOCK ON ANY DOOR — Columbia 1949
CHICAGO DEADLINE — Paramount 1949
BATTLEGROUND — MGM 1949
ADVENTURE IN BALTIMORE (Baltimore Escapade) — RKO Radio 1949
THE JUDGE STEPS OUT (Indian Summer) — RKO Radio 1949
THE HAPPY YEARS (You're Only Young Twice, Dink Stover) —
    MGM 1950
TRIPLE TROUBLE — Monogram 1950
PERFECT STRANGERS — Warner Bros. 1950
SINGING GUNS — Republic 1950
KANSAS RAIDERS — Universal 1950
PRETTY BABY — Warner Bros. 1950

THE NEXT VOICE YOU HEAR — MGM 1950
ACROSS THE WIDE MISSOURI — MGM 1951
DISC JOCKEY — Allied Artists 1951
DOUBLE DYNAMITE — RKO Radio 1951
WESTWARD THE WOMEN — MGM 1951
WOMAN OF THE NORTH COUNTRY — Republic 1952
HANS CHRISTIAN ANDERSEN — RKO Radio 1952
THIS WOMAN IS DANGEROUS — Warner Bros. 1952
AND NOW TOMORROW — Westminster Productions 1952
THE WAC FROM WALLA WALLA — Republic 1952
MY MAN AND I — MGM 1952
ROSE OF CIMARRON — 20th Century-Fox 1952
SOMEBODY LOVES ME — Paramount 1952
TARGET — RKO Radio 1952
MEET ME AT THE FAIR — Universal-International 1952
ISLAND IN THE SKY — Warner Bros. 1953
MARRY ME AGAIN — RKO Radio 1953
SUPERMAN IN EXILE — 20th Century-Fox 1954 [comprised of 1953
    Superman TV episodes]
THE HIGH AND THE MIGHTY — Warner Bros. 1954
DUFFY OF SAN QUENTIN — Warner Bros. 1954
THE STEEL CAGE — United Artists 1954
RAILS INTO LARAMIE — Universal 1954
THE GIRL RUSH — Paramount 1955
APACHE AMBUSH (Renegade Roundup) — Columbia 1955
GOOD-BYE, MY LADY — Warner Bros. 1956
SPRING REUNION — United Artists 1957
GUNSIGHT RIDGE — United Artists 1957
DEAD RINGER — Warner Bros. 1964
LAW OF THE LAWLESS — Paramount 1964
BLACK SPURS — Paramount 1965
APACHE UPRISING — Paramount 1966
THE GHOST AND MR. CHICKEN — Universal 1966
BUCKSKIN — Paramount 1968
ONE MORE TRAIN TO ROB — Universal 1971
PICKUP ON 101 — American International Pictures 1972
CAPONE — 20th Century-Fox 1975
ESCAPE TO WITCH MOUNTAIN — Disney-Buena Vista 1975
THE APPLE DUMPLING GANG — Disney-Buena Vista 1975
GRIFFIN AND PHOENIX: A LOVE STORY — ABC Circle 1976 [TV movie]
THE BASTARD (The Kent Chronicles) — Operation Prime Time-Universal
    1978 [TV movie]
EVERY WHICH WAY BUT LOOSE — Warner Bros. 1978
THE APPLE DUMPLING GANG RIDES AGAIN —
    Disney-Buena Vista 1979

Index

ORDER FORM

Please send the following books:

Qty   Amount

___ *Reel Characters* paperback @ $9.95   _____
___ *Reel Characters* hardcover @ $19.95   _____
___ *Spike Jones and his City Slickers* paperback @ $14.95   _____
___ *Spike Jones and his City Slickers* hardcover @ $29.95   _____

                                           Total for books   _____
            Postage: add $1.50 first book; 50¢ each additional _____
                  California residents please add 6% sales tax _____
                         Amount enclosed (U.S. funds)   _____

Ship to:

_____

_____

_____

Please send ordering information:
___ Laurel and Hardy: *The Magic Behind the Movies*
___ Laurel and Hardy music tracks (audio cassette)
___ *The Spike Jones Song Book*
___ Spike Jones rarities (audio cassette)

IF THIS IS A LIBRARY BOOK, PLEASE PHOTOCOPY THIS PAGE.

SATISFACTION GUARANTEED OR PURCHASE PRICE REFUNDED.

(m)oonstone press

P.O. Box 142, Beverly Hills, CA 90213